MW01288889

We All Leak Eventually

Hope you enjoy

Larry

by

LARRY CASTRIOTTA

Copyright © 2015 LARRY CASTRIOTTA

All rights reserved. Use of any part of this publication without prior written consent of the author(s) is an infringement of the copyright law.

Acknowledgements

Writing a book is an epic effort with equal parts of elation and frustration. My wife Martha has shared both emotions with me in huge measures. You will notice that quite a few of these stories were inspired by her and involve her. Thank you Martha for making my life more interesting and for putting up with me while I worked on this opus.

I also wish to thank my editor and friend Alexis Powers, a wonderful writer in her own right. Alexis is the reason this book is written. Without her enthusiastic support and encouragement I would never have undertaken this project.

Valerie Howard did a wonderful job on the book cover. Thank you for your creativity

Lastly I want to thank the Oro Valley, (Pima County), Library for sponsoring Alexis's Writer's Motivational Workshop. The workshop provides a safe environment for would be authors to test out their writing skills and to listen to the work of other writers.

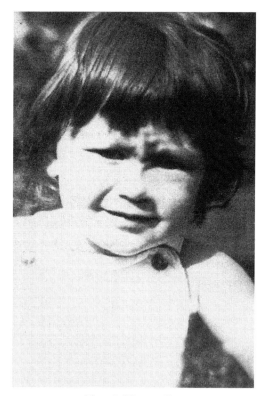

Me at 18 months.
I had this hairdo 15 years before the Beatles!

Foreword

The stories contained in this book are my version of what happened, a "Fictionalized Memoir." It is fictionalized not because it is "made up," but because no one can remember things accurately from day to day, let alone through seven decades.

The story about Tweet's is a good example. I remember it as Tweet being in the kitchen. Tweets wife and family think I may have remembered Tweet's father. It doesn't matter. The essence is correct.

I would like to thank the family of Tweet Balzano for providing the picture of Tweet and his dad.

Some situations have been stretched for the sake of humor. Those are easily identifiable. The direction of this book is to look at events I was involved in through a humorous or interesting prism.

Martha and I have had amazing adventures. We have also faced various problems. Martha likes to say, "When you're old and gray and sitting in a rocker on the porch, you won't remember that five star hotel stay where everything was perfect. You will remember that time you went to New Zealand and did a Bungee Jump or almost got killed driving on the wrong side of the street."

The setting for a good part of this book is my home town, Bristol, Rhode Island. When I was growing up the population was 12,000. Today I believe it has doubled. Many towns and cities have experienced great changes, but Bristol has maintained most of its charm. Somewhat sketchy areas of town have been beautifully restored or "gentrified." Most of the classic historical buildings have been preserved and they tell a beautiful history of the town. My last visit there reinforced my view that the spirit and energy that made Bristol a wonderful place to grow up or live in was still there.

The Catholic Church is the subject of much discussion in this book. My spiritual journey has led me away from Catholicism to Unitarian Universalism. Most of the stories about the church are from my growing up years. I also relate some of the issues I dealt with getting married to a non-Catholic. Thirdly, I take a look at the impact Boomers have had on the Church.

I describe my interactions with the Church, its bureaucracy and the cultural issues the Church faces. If you are a devout Catholic, a Sunday only Catholic or an Easter and Christmas only Catholic, I am happy for you. I respect your beliefs and acknowledge that the Church does many good things and helps millions of people but you have to admit it leaves itself wide open to a lot of humor.

The pictures in this book are not of the highest quality. There are two basic reasons for this: Many of the originals are very old and not in the best condition. The second reason is that I apparently suck as a photographer.

I hope you read this book with the attitude that you are sharing the life of a man who has done many interesting things while having a great time in life and who loves to look at things a differently.

Chapter One

On the Bubble Generation

Here's the deal. All my life every social commentator, economist, marketer and damn futurist, (the only profession I know of with a lower accuracy rating than weather forecasters) has focused on the "baby boomers."

Daddy came home from the war with a tremendous hard-on and had his way with Mommy a few too many times over the next ten years. The next thing you know the adult population of the country is making cootchie-coo noises over this new crowd of ca-ca factories.

With the older child shunted aside for the new baby, my generation watched with growing hatred as the new kid got all the attention. Yup, we made the mistake of being born between 1940 and 1945. Son-of-a-bitch! We were the "On the Bubble Generation."

If we had been smart enough to have been born earlier, we would have had the opportunity to start our careers early enough so we could laud it over this new bunch of snot-nosed kids when they entered the workforce.

So there we were, the prototypical middle child: A selfish older sibling who grabbed all the candy and wouldn't share. Then we have our nemesis who is a precocious little brat whose shit was viewed as gold bars by a war machine with no war to fight. What's a generation to do? Break out the world's largest jar of Vaseline and assume the position!

Next thing you know this bunch of jokers starts breaking all the rules we had to follow.

1. If you go to college, you are supposed to get married as soon as you graduate if not sooner. That way you can have sex legally and hopefully, regularly. If you don't go to college or go into the service, the rules are the same. The timeline is the only thing that changes.

Not this bunch of jokers. As soon as they hit puberty they start screwing around. Tiffany isn't saying, "No. No. I'm a good girl. Not till we're married." She's out asking guys if they want to "get it on." She isn't even particular who she does it with. This is called FREE LOVE.

Hell, it was never free in my generation. It wasn't even on sale! In my day it took about 532 dates, a thousand drinks, tons of Beach Blanket Bingo movies and a lot of holding hands. Then you might be able to get a few good French kisses and cop a feel before Mary starts with the "No, No" routine.

2. Your government knows best! They wouldn't lie to you so just be quiet!

The President has a lot more information than we do. We shouldn't question what he does.

The boomers didn't get that memo. When they weren't screwing their brains out, they decided that we shouldn't be in Vietnam. College campuses erupted with protests about the war, civil rights, abortions and bad food. Anything that could get them arrested was fair game for a protest. In addition to the government, this group took on anything that smelled vaguely of authority.

3. Don't take any drugs. You will become a heroin addict. If you smoke marijuana you will want to take heroin and there is no turning back from that!

Pass the joint while I cover this point. If you want to understand this issue, go see a few Cheech and Chong movies. On top of that, the lost generation had a new hero; a Harvard professor no less, Timothy Leary. The hell with doobies, we're going to drop some acid. LSD became the rage with these young idiots. They were all "tripping."

While this was going on, I followed all the rules. Right after college when I was 21, I got married, settled into a monogamous life, got a job, had two kids and bought a house, while feeling very superior to those value-less dodos.

At the time they were all randomly mating and protesting whatever the cause of the day was, I was grilling burgers in the back yard and drinking Scotch and Soda with other conventional couples. Comparatively, we were boring as hell!!

How did this all start?

To begin with, I was born. I mention this because it seems everyone thinks the boomers' parents invented sex. It's true, billions of people had already said, "Was it good for you, too?" long before 1946. Anyway, I entered the world on May 6, 1945. If Mom could have let me out a few days earlier, I could have been born the day Hitler got out of the canoe. What a claim to fame! The only cool thing that ever happened on May 6 was Babe Ruth hitting his first home run for the Yankees, back in 1920.

After that inauspicious start, I soon learned that I was the last of four kids born to a talented Irish/English R.N. and a first generation Italian jack-of-all-trades. The oldest offspring was my brother Lou. Mom said he was a genius. To prove her objectivity she had him tested, and damned if he wasn't. Next came "The Twins." That's what they were called: not Janice and Joyce -"The Twins." The only reason these two creatures were put on this earth was to torment me. I'm convinced that they are living proof that God has a dark sense of humor.

We lived in a suburb of Providence, Rhode Island, which in itself is strange, since everybody in Massachusetts thinks Rhode Island is a suburb of Boston. By the way, that's another thing that gripes me. Why are the Boomers credited with the creation of the Suburbs? Suburbs existed long before the Baby Boomers. See, the word is a contraction of two words- sub and urban. Put them together and you have a word that means an area less than urban. In other words, it ain't "citified."

Be that as it may, Bristol, Rhode Island is a peninsula of land on the east side of Narragansett Bay that served as Newport's main route back to the real world. Growing up in this small town of 12,000 people was a lesson in history. In addition, it was a wonderful place to cultivate an inferiority complex. Nobody ever came to Bristol. They went through it, or left it, but never came to it, except the British, or on the FOURTH OF JULY. I'll explain about the FOURTH later.

The British sailed into Bristol Harbor in the pre -revolutionary years and routinely bombed the crap out of the town. This somewhat unfriendly gesture was prompted by the fact that some of the worthy residents were engaged in the slave and rum-running business. They also didn't think too much of King George's newer taxes.

Despite the British over-reaction, there are still plenty of houses dating back to the late 17th and early 18th centuries. All duly noted with bronze plaques in front of them placed by the blue-blooded elite of the Bristol Historical Society.

A friend of mine lived in one of these old houses. By the mid-1950's, it had developed into a mini-slum, was subdivided and rented out. But it still had its plaque! Aside from being old, this dive had the distinction of having been hit by a British cannonball, and the ball was still inside the wall of the house! We could go into a closet in the hallway and look up to see the cannonball embedded in the timbers.

God forbid we should ever try to touch it. That would have caused a cataclysmic rage on the part of those anointed to protect the historic legacy of the town. Amazingly, we believed that somehow they would know the moment one of our grubby fingers approached within an inch of this relic. Then they would come swooping down on us and without due process we would be permanently sentenced to Sockanosett, the State's bad-boy detention center.

Looking back, it seems to me that very few of these old houses were occupied by families with children. I guess I thought they all belonged to old people that gave birth to adult children, who later became old people and took over the house and gave birth to more adult offspring, etc., etc.

The houses were never owned by people with names like Russo, Squatrito or Benevides. It was always Evans, Perry (yep, as in the Commodore) or DeWolf. These were families that looked down on members of the DAR as carpetbaggers.

Making a Buck

In the mid-fifties, nobody would hire a kid unless they were 16 years old. My folks didn't believe in allowances, so if I wanted some money I had to find a way to earn it. The easiest way for a kid living near the ocean would be to dig for quahogs, also called little necks, which are hard shelled clams.

There were several spots in Bristol where you could dig for them. My favorite was in a tidal pond in what is now Colt State Park. At low tide you would walk into the water about up to your knees with your long tined rake and a burlap bag. You would swing the rake into the pond bottom and bring up a bunch of mud. Then you sifted through it, hoping you would find one or two. If you lucked out and hit a nest, you could fill out pretty quick.

Because of the tide, you only had a limited amount of time so you couldn't go out of the water for a lunch break. What we would do is crack a couple of quahogs together and eat them.

After a hard day, we would sell our bounty to Quito's shellfish. He paid us between eight and fifteen cents a pound. A good day in the water was worth three to five bucks. Not bad for the late fifties.

Another way we made money is spearing eels. Bob Evans had a boat so went out at night. Bob would row slowly and I would hang over the transom of the boat with a flashlight in one hand and a trident spear in the other. We got around a dollar apiece for them. My grandmother loved them so I would always take her a couple. She would clean them then stuff them with stale bread soaked in olive oil and black olive bits and, of course, garlic. Then she would bake them. I can smell her kitchen now.

Nanna lived alone in her house next to the store she and her husband ran in the twenties, thirties and forties. Although the house was old, it had been updated. There was a gas stove and a heating system, but she had no use for either of these new-fangled contraptions. She favored her big, old black cast iron stove fired by coal. That was what she preferred to cook on and heat her house with. There was a delicious smell to her house as she always had orange or lemon rinds cooking on the stove top.

Every day at lunch time, I would go to her house and get a bucket of coal from the cellar for her. My reward was whatever I wanted for lunch she would cook. Dad and Lou would also come for lunch and this amazing woman would make us whatever we wanted. "Luigi che volgo a ierie? (What do you want tomorrow?) "Pepper and eggs, Nanna"...no problem. Dad wanted meatballs and spaghetti...no problem. Larry wanted lasagna...no problem. We all got what we wanted. Love by kitchen!

I could never do anything wrong in Nanna's eyes. I was her favorite. This wizened small woman, with gray hair stood a mighty five feet. She never asked for anything for herself, but if she wanted something for one of her friends she was a giant.

The family would gather on Sunday afternoons for dinner at our house or at Zizi's. Invariably we would end up in the living room discussing family happenings or political issues. I would always end up on the couch next to Nanna and she would find some way to stroke or tickle me; on my arm, back, thigh, neck, whatever.

I remember thinking that if I acknowledge what she was doing she might stop, but if I didn't let her know I loved it, she would be unhappy and stop. What's a kid to do? What I eventually learned was that she would never stop until she got tired because she knew I loved it.

I believe I learned my first lessons in true love from this woman.

Dad, Nana and me
Relaxing after a big Sunday meal

Chapter Two

Religion

The non Euro ethnic people living in our town all went to their own churches. Their choices were: First Congregational, Presbyterian, Trinity Church, or St. Michaels, the latter two being Protestant. I always wanted to join one of their churches. I figured if my Dad switched us to one of them we would automatically get a new car, and Mom would get a lot of new jewelry!

But no, we kept going to Our Lady of Mount Carmel. This was the Catholic Church for the Italians. We had St. Mary's for the Irish, and St. Elizabeth's for the Portuguese. Tommy Eisenstadt's family had to travel all the way to Providence for the synagogue.

The way I looked at it, the blue bloods may have it made here on earth, but they were sure going to fry in hell when they died. They didn't have priests, except for Trinity Church, but he was married. They didn't have nuns, and their pastors spoke in English when they were on the altar. Our guys always spoke in some gibberish called Latin, which is obviously what God spoke.

Here's a popular joke: Mr. Smith dies and St. Peter is showing him around. He takes him to the first door and slides a little window aside. "This is where the Protestants are. They're a quiet bunch but you can see they're very happy." He takes them to the next door and peeks into the window. "These are the Jews. Very prayerful and happy for their deliverance."

Before approaching the next door, St. Peter admonished Mr. Smith, "You will have to be very quiet at this next one. It belongs to the Catholics, and they think they are the only ones here."

The Catholic priests were called "Father." We had Father Joseph, Monsignor Lynch and Father Luis. These other guys were Pastor White, Canon Delbert W. Tilsley, or Reverend James House.

Then there was Father John N. Sinclair from Trinity Church. I kept waiting for our priest to have him arrested. Not only did he call himself a priest, he even wore a Roman collar, and he knew Latin. Like I said, he was married! On top of that he had four kids. The two youngest, David and Deane, were my best friends. I mean, okay, you're a priest and you want to get married— fine—but no "doing it" with your wife!

* * *

Our Lady of Mount Carmel was officially a Mission church, which meant, at that time, all the priests came from Italy out of the Carmelite Seminary. Two of the pastors made big impressions on me. The first was Father Joseph Sorzano. He must not have been tall because I remember being taller than him even when I was seven. He was as bald as a cue ball with a big round head. Thinking about him now, he must have been about 65 years old.

I can truly say that I never saw the man smile, NEVER. Even when he was rapturously talking about God, he did it in a loud angry voice with a deep scowl on his face.

Most of his sermons had little to do with the gospel and a lot to do with money. We had the regular Sunday collection. We had the fairly regular collection for Bishop McVinney's

Diocesan debt reduction. Then we would have any number of special collections for missionary work, the poor people of Italy, the starving children of Korea, the retired nuns and priests , etc. etc. etc.

None of the above should be confused with Father Joseph's ranting about donations needed for the Altar Society or the School Building Fund or the Church Restoration Fund. Nor should we forget the raffle tickets for the benefit of the Holy Name Society, the White Elephant Sale being run by the CYO or the ham and bean dinner sponsored by the Knights of Columbus.

Most of these events took place in the 50's and early 60's. My Dad and Mom never made a lot of money, but we always had decent clothes and plenty of food, even when Dad was unemployed. But the financial burden of being a Catholic seemed a bit excessive. Even if you gave your fair share, Father Joseph would get up in that pulpit and harangue us for 20 minutes. Being told that you're selfish, uncaring and cheap is bad enough, but when delivered at 90 decibels in broken English by a sawed off Mussolini look-a-like, it's damned scary.

Dad took this crap for years. Finally, he lost it. The church year started right after Easter. Each family member was given a box of Sunday donation cards plus appropriate extras for the Holy Days of Obligation. You earned the obligation to "give" as soon as you entered instruction for First Communion. At Mass each Sunday you put your money in the envelope, sealed it and put it in the collection basket.

Instead of using his envelopes, Dad put cash in the basket. He felt that it wasn't anybody's business how much he gave and the only reason for the envelopes was to keep track of who gave what. Considering his means and the times, I thought he was pretty generous.

Shortly after Easter one year, Father Joseph was up in the pulpit banging away on his favorite theme that "the measure of your Faith is in the numbers." He was so into that I thought he was going to stroke out on us right then and there. But then it happened—the closest thing to a smile I ever saw from the man.

As he directed the ushers to hand out the little books, he got this strange smug look on his face. Sure enough, they were keeping score. It was a list of every parishioner and exactly how much they had donated to the Church and their beloved Pastor. Next to the Castriotta name was the princely total of $14.25, the sum total of the nickels and dimes from me and my sibling's envelopes.

Dad was apoplectic. When he got pissed, he cursed in Italian. But curse he did right in the pew. Starting softly, he began picking up volume. At about the time he could be heard at the front of the Church, he started repeating himself, then stood up and went storming out of the Church.

He hung around the side door until the mass was over. Father Joseph came out and Dad started cursing again, this time in English. I think he wanted the gathering crowd of parishioners to be clear that he wasn't congratulating the good priest on his sermon.

"Who the f***   do you think you are? What I give to this Church is my own damned business! What my friends give is theirs! What gives you the right blah, blah, blah"

This went on for a minute or two, Father Joe starts to sense that the crowd is on Dad's side. The little runt starts getting smaller. Then he mumbles something and turns and runs for the Parish House. Within weeks, Father Joseph is history.

Enter Father Mario Tardivo. What a breath of fresh air. This was not a tyrannical, ugly little man. This was a relatively young, approximately 45, vibrant, likeable, worldly man. People were actually allowed to laugh in church when he made jokes from the pulpit. He never yelled, not even during his sermons, which meant that for the first time in years, Dad could get a decent snooze in on a Sunday morning. With this change, we actually looked forward to going to mass.

HE EVEN CAME TO OUR HOUSE!! I mean, like a guest. About once a month, he came over for dinner. Bourbon was his drink. Unbelievably, not only did he play Keno with us, but he left his own jar of pennies at our house for the next game. What the heck was going on? Next you're going to tell me this guy farted once in a while, just like regular people!

That's not all. I was always told that priests take vows of poverty, chastity, and obedience.

Poverty: They have no money and no personal possessions other than the necessities provided by the church.

Chastity: No fooling around with women ever and no playing with yourself.

Obedience: When your Superiors tell you to jump, you ask how high.

If Father Mario were a baseball player he would have a great batting average of 333. Of the three vows, I think he got the chastity thing right.

Poverty:

In addition to the Parish car, he bought a war surplus Jeep. If that weren't enough, he bought a helicopter. He learned to fly one as an Army Chaplain in WWII, Periodically, he would take the altar boys or a bunch of us from CYO for an outing which usually included a visit to Supreme Ice Cream Dairy and a helicopter ride. He also wore regular people's clothes. I think that's when I first realized that the Roman Collar wasn't actually part of a priest's skin.

Obedience:

There are a lot of little stories about Father Mario not doing exactly as he was directed. Like not stopping all Latin masses after the Vatican Council or delaying the turning around of the altar until he was threatened with disciplinary action.

It wasn't that he was lazy or against the changes. He was trying to serve his flock. Each Euro-ethnic Catholic Church had a substantial group of Black Widows. These were women, generally born in the old country, who had lost their husbands. Most of them spoke broken, if any, English. On the day their men died their whole wardrobe turned black and they developed an overwhelming need to go to mass every day.

The daily mass at 7:30 each morning was a standard Latin mass but the sermon and all announcements were delivered in Italian. This was how the sisterhood found out if its number was growing or shrinking.

Generally of advanced age, these women had been devout, unquestioning Catholics for many decades. With their early schooling in the old country, they believed in the saintliness of their priests, even Father Sorzano. They were led to believe that the priests were endowed with magic-like powers. How else could you explain Transubstantiation to illiterate peasants?

Along comes the Vatican Council and says no more Latin, and let's turn the altar around to share the service with our Parishioners. The last thing the Black Widows want is have the mumbo jumbo become plain old Italian. It wasn't for them to see or understand the magic the priest was performing. It would destroy the myth!

Well, Father Mario to the rescue! After protracted debates he came up with a clever solution. He instructed the Black Widows to keep their heads bowed and to say the rosary while he was performing the mass. And instead of doing the Latin portion in Italian, he did it in English, which most of them didn't understand any better than Latin. Everybody was happy.

Fish on Friday

The happiest guy in my hometown was the fish truck driver on Thursday and Friday. Any other day of the week and nobody knew him from Adam. He could park in your driveway, take his best looking fish out of the truck, carry it to your door, recite it's royal bloodlines and give you recipes to turn it into the most divine taste you ever had and he would be told to get lost.

But on Thursday and Friday, he was the "Man." He would pull up to the curb somewhere near the middle of the block and toot his horn.

Housewives would come storming out of their houses running, begging him to sell them that last piece of carp. They would call in all their chits, "Hey, you sonufabitch, don't you remember when I bought that rotten scungili from you on a Tuesday three years ago?"

What could possibly cause this schizophrenia? The Catholic Church! You see, to honor Christ's death on the cross, Pope Peter the First decided that everyone should eat fish on Fridays...well kinda. He didn't actually come out and say that, but it was the next best thing. What he really said was, "Don't eat meat." Aside from going vegetarian, what other choices did people have? FISH!

Now follow me close here. What was the occupation of most of the Apostles? One was an accountant. He was taken care of when the income tax was instituted.

Wasn't another into water? Hey, baptism and holy water! Another guy was a teacher. Where do you think tenure originated?

But the rest of them were fishermen!

Chapter Three

How the Boomers changed the Church

As you probably have already figured out, I don't have the greatest relationship with the Catholic church. Don't get me wrong, I admire the hell out of that institution.

Popular Joke: A young Jew, shortly after witnessing his first Catholic mass, goes back to his rabbi and tells him that he is converting. Not only is he converting, he is going to become a priest!

"But why?" asks the rabbi.

The young man responds, "First the priest gets dressed in beautiful silk robes and stands on the altar."

"But we have fine, if plain, robes as well," answers the holy man.

"Yes, but then he goes up to the altar and admires all his gold bowls and chalices, and teases the congregation by holding them up for all to see," the young Jew continues.

"Gold and silver are not the most important things in the world bubbala," says the rabbi

"Ah, yes, your holiness, but then he makes himself a snack of bread and wine. And when he is finished two young boys come over and wash his hands."

"This cannot be good reason for you to leave your faith."

"Oh, no! It is what comes next! He turns back to the congregation and with his hands outstretched he exhorts the people. I don't know what he says as it is in a different language. But the people must know, because five men start walking down the aisle collecting money from them. Then these plates of money are brought to the priest and he smiles. Oy, Rabbi, what a business. How did we ever pass this one up?"

Now don't go getting the idea that I am cynical. After all, I know there is more to the church than just passing the plate on Sunday morning.

There is after all, in the USA at least, the non-profit status, and the tax exempt properties worth billions, as well as the bully pulpit, (literally), to influence legislators all across the country. At the same time, they don't have to worry about following the strictures of the constitution of the country that houses and protects them.

How's that you say? When was the last time you saw a woman saying mass? How many women bishops or cardinals do you know? Have you ever compared the pay checks or living conditions of priests versus nuns? Does anybody say, "Bless me, sister, for I have sinned"? Where are the radical feminists on these issues?

The Catholic Church has changed. By sheer force of numbers, the boomers managed to put the fear of God, so to speak, into the Catholic Church.

When I grew up only the "pure," or those thought to be "pure," were ever allowed on the altar. Priests and altar boys, that's it! Only the priest was allowed to touch the Body and Blood of Christ. At First Communion instruction you were drilled on the proper reverence for the host. The priest is ordained, and he can touch IT. "But, Sister Mary, what if he drops it out of his hands and it falls in my lap?" DON'T YOU DARE TOUCH IT! YOU ARE NOT ORDAINED! "Okay, okay, just asking." Now they come around and hand it to you like they're passing out business cards.

Okay, okay, there is much to admire about the Catholic church. In some ways it has been very responsive to the meaningful needs of its flock.

As an example: When I was growing up you had to go to mass every Sunday. Every Sunday and all Holy Days of Obligation. That meant between the hours of 12:00 a.m. to 11:59.59 p.m. If you didn't, it was a mortal sin, generally good for five years to life in purgatory if forgiven before you croak or eternal damnation if unforgiven.

Well, along came the Boomers, and guess what? "Hey, Padre, I don't mind having to come to church every week. Heck, it's gotten to be a really good time what with the folk masses and all that, but can't we be a little more flexible about this?

"See, it's really rough to go out on Saturday night and get really stupid and then have to get up for that noon Sunday High Mass. Nothing personal, Father, but you're no Pavarotti. Besides, those Lutherans get to go whenever they feel like it, and they have their own insurance company."

Well, one of those three day Popes back in the 70's says, "No problem." Now you can go to mass on Saturday and then go out and get ripped. That is responsive.

I'm sure that part of the deal was that all those poor bastards that were frying in hell for missing mass in the prior two thousand years got full pardons and were given their wings.

Recently, I went to a Catholic wedding. Surprisingly, I wasn't sure who the priest was. I had a pretty good idea it was the guy sitting in the back and to the side of the pulpit because he administered the vows. There was a steady parade of people coming out of the pews and going up to the pulpit to read this or that, or to deliver some important mini-sermon to the newlyweds. Hell, they practically needed a damned traffic cop to prevent mix-ups.

Hasn't the priest got it easy enough? Six days a week he does a 45 minute service. On Sunday, maybe he does three. Occasionally, he officiates at a Saturday wedding or a mid-week funeral. The rest of the time it's Lions Club luncheons or golfing dates. Is the strain of this schedule so tough that we gotta do the services for him, too?

Another thing the McDonald's generation is still lobbying for is drive-up windows. You pull in alongside the Basilica with the Flying Arches. If you haven't had time to get to confession, you stop at the first window and yell to the priest behind the screen, "Hey Father, I screwed up on a few things. Can I cop a pass?"

"Sure, no problem. Have a nice day!" says the rapid religion reverend. Up to the next window and order two real host deals and three kiddie meal deals; two hosts and three Papal Blessings.

Recently they added the Arch Angel Deluxe deal, two hosts with sacramental wine. Some churches will offer you a few choices: Plain, Onion, or Blueberry flavored hosts with or without cream cheese. Right below the window is a box for your weekly contribution.

One more bitch about the Catholic Church. In 1966 I got engaged to a Congregationalist. Well, you would have thought

I just confessed to 20 rape-murders. First my mother says she won't come to the wedding unless it's performed by a Catholic priest. Then my future in-laws insist on having one of their clerics be part of the act. The new pastor at Mt Carmel says, "No problem. Just have Ottilie convert." Nice solution, but she says, "No way."

We finally come up with a compromise. Otti and I will get married at the non-denominational chapel at Boston University (we both graduated from there) by a Catholic priest from the Boston Archdiocese, and invite her pastor to participate *in* the service. If my parents or hers don't like it, they don't have to come: piss on 'em! Great solution.

Well, almost. We couldn't possibly imagine all the roadblocks a determined, out of date, monolith like the Catholic church can put up. Representing that institution was another out of -date monolith, Richard Cardinal Cushing.

At the age of about 80, he was literally a god in Boston. He never used the Sumner Tunnel to get to the airport, he just walked across the harbor. Every Boston politician was fighting to see who could get their nose further up his ass. One good public word from the Cardinal, and you were in. One bad word and you were as dead as Kelsey's nuts.

Cushing's concept of the Catholic religion was that you went to confession every Saturday and told the priest all your real or imagined misdeeds. He gave you absolution and you went to mass and Communion the next day. You didn't eat meat on Fridays or during Lent. Whenever possible, you sent your kids to the growing number of parochial schools, an inordinate number of which were named after the Cardinal or his favorite saints.

You listened attentively to his frequent pastoral letters being read from the pulpit, and you always voted for Roosevelt. Oh, that's right, he isn't around anymore.

We were told that Otti and I would need to go through five weeks of counseling sessions at St Cecilia's Church in Boston, and Otti would have to do a few more so that she understood the requirement that she would raise any children as Catholics. We went through all this crap and thought we were home free.

The last weapon in the Cardinal's arsenal was to announce to us two weeks before the wedding that the priest assigned to do our wedding would not be available for some mysterious reason and none others were available.

I was royally pissed and wanted to take it out on someone. I waltzed into the Newman House on Bay State Road looking for a fight. The Newman House is kind of like a Fraternity/Sorority for Catholics on campus. This was in mid-July and we had scheduled the wedding for the 30th. I was met there by an affable young man about 30 years old.

I told him my story. It turns out he was a priest from the Baltimore Diocese who was taking summer classes at Boston U. He said, "No problem. Cushing can't do anything to me. I'll marry you."

So we ended up with a Catholic priest officiating, assisted by a Congregational minister and a Jewish organist in a non-denominational chapel!

Chapter Four

The Twins

Janice and Joyce: That's the way they came out. First Janice and then Joyce. So if you ever said their names together you always said Janice and Joyce, never Joyce and Janice. But you almost never used their names, it was always the Twins. "Larry, tell the Twins it's time to eat." "Lou, the Twins need new clothes." "Mom, I saw the Twins smoking at Gloria Brown's house."

Now these two girls were not identical. Not in the least. But they created a single persona that I, the younger brother, had to deal with. If I were a paranoid individual, I would believe that the only time these two combined their personality forces was against me. Trust me, l have enough evidence to support this theory.

Janice, the pioneer of the two, was the first down the birth canal. The struggle to widen the pathway for her trailing sibling took its toll. She was born small and stayed skinny until after she had a couple of kids. We're talking major league skinny at 5'5" and 85 pounds, if she were retaining water. Dark hair and dark eyes, favoring my father's side of the family.

Joyce, sliding down the birth canal behind her sister, yelling "Wheee, this is gonna be a great ride! Anybody got any food? The chow in there was getting kinda old. Hey, Dad, Janice said I should ask if we can borrow the car when we turn 16."

At about the same height as her sister, Joyce was always a little bit overweight. Not fat by any means, just a little plump. Unfortunately, standing next to Janice she looked like Mama Cass Elliot. Blue-eyed and brown haired she, like me, favored Mom's side of the family.

The twins were born two years before me which gave them just enough time to get the lay of the land and set up a few booby traps for their little brother. Let me give you a couple of examples.

Being the "baby" of the family, I was usually the first one to go to bed and I would fall asleep like a shot. One of the twins would slip into my room and slide under my bed. Then she would very gently push up on my bed, gradually increasing the intensity.

While this was going on, the other twin would be making weird noises like a ghost.

This would continue until I woke up screaming in terror or the girls broke out laughing, usually both.

As I got older, their torments became more cerebral. I went to a Catholic high school in Providence. This meant I had to get up very early to catch the bus. Most of the year, it was pitch dark when I left in the morning.

The twins would wait until I had been asleep for an hour or so and then make my alarm go off. They would hide in their room and sneak looks at me while I went through my morning routine, got dressed, and went downstairs to make breakfast. This farce continued until I noticed my parents were in the family room watching T.V.

The twins were two years older than me but I was only one year behind them in school since I got an early start. As a result, I knew all their friends pretty well and went to a lot of their parties. In fact, I was the designated date when one of their friends didn't want to ask somebody to the prom or some other important function.

That meant I was drinking beer well before my time!

This continued when the girls graduated high school and developed new friends at their colleges.

In Bristol there was a legendary institution known as Tweet's. It was run by a gentleman named Tweet Balzano. The original building was literally an oversized chicken coop. Additional improvements were a couple of shaky lean-tos with outside walls of chicken wire with a couple of rough board long tables. Light bulbs hung from the rafters holding up the tin roof. In the rearmost lean-to there were two bulbs covering an area 20 feet long and 10 or 12 feet wide.

Tweet was a great man. He treated everyone the same. We were all family.

Tweet made the greatest hoagies: meatballs, sausage, chorizo and peppers, Italian cold cuts. You could also get steamed clams or little neck quahogs (hard shell clams) on the half shell.

When you walked into the place, the kitchen area was off to the right and there was Tweet making hoagies. He was standing there greeting people while he worked. "Hey, little Lorenzo (me), what the hell you doin' here? You 12 years old yet? I gave him the finger and he laughed. Actually I was 16 at the time.

Tweet didn't dress like a normal chef or even a cook. He was dressed in a guinea tee shirt. Now they call them wife beater tees. It was an undershirt with thin shoulder straps and no sleeves. So there was a lot of hair showing on his back, arms and underarms. The way it worked was let's say two of us came in together: Tweet would say, "Whatyall have?"

"Meatball for me and a Italian sausage for my date."

'Yeah I'll bet," he'd guffaw.

So he'd grab a loaf of bread for one sandwich and stick it between his arm and his side, up near his armpit. He would pick up another loaf and start making one of the hoagies. I didn't want to know which one because then I would know which one was the armpit special.

Janice's friends were from Providence and loved going to Tweet's because nobody ever checked IDs. Hell, at 16 I could get as much beer as I wanted. We would take over the back lean-to and drink Narragansett ponies for hours on end.

The evil twins plotting against me already!

Right after this picture they pushed me down the stairs.

Tweet's Dad Papa John

Which one made the "Armpit Special"

Chapter Five

The Fourth of July

Bristol, Rhode Island, not only has the longest continuously running Independence Day celebration in the country but it is the largest. The party is a week-long event. The centerpiece of the festivities is a parade that lasts longer than the Macy's Thanksgiving Day Parade.

The celebration brings bands not only from all over the east coast but some from the midwest. The Mummers from Philadelphia appear, as well as Drum and Bugle Corps from all over New England and New York.

Each year there were dignitaries and beauty queens riding in convertibles. Guess who got to drive them? Guys like me.

I got my driver's license in May and on July 4th I was driving a brand new 1961 Ford Galaxy convertible! YES! We all got ferried up to Tasca Ford in East Providence and were given a car to drive back to Bristol so that some bimbo could sit in the back seat and give that phony wave for a couple of hours.

Then we had a couple of hours before we had to get the cars back. We would ride around town, go to Colt Drive and have fun showing off!

What a kick!

The celebration would have a carnival, usually Kid Hopes, on the Town Common. A greasy pole climb, talent show contests, a Block Dance, amateur boxing, fireman's muster competitions and a huge fireworks display.

Any normal Fourth would swell our town's population ten-fold. That meant you had to stay in the next town out, Warren, and hope you could get a parking spot within one or two miles from the parade route. In the Bi-Centennial year we heard claims that there were as many as 350,000 people in town for the parade.

Putting on this kind of production is no small feat and it is managed by the Bristol Fourth Of July Committee. Just like the Rose Bowl Parade they always have a Grand Marshall.

Being named GM is a huge honor and from my memory it seemed like they almost always picked worthy citizens to honor. That meant that the honoree had to fork out a ton of money to put on a party for the Committee and all visiting royalty and dignitaries.

One year there was a GM that really pissed Dad off.

To better understand, let me give you a little background.

My Grandfather was born in Italy and migrated to the U.S. He married and he and my grandmother had my father. Financially he did very well and when my dad was five years old they returned to Italy. Around 1921 they returned to the U.S. and Nonno opened up a corner grocery store that also had a gas pump. It was the first ESSO station in Rhode Island. The store prospered and my grandfather made a comfortable living.

Bristol was a town with a large immigrant population. A third of the town's residents were Italians, almost all of which were from the Manfredonia area, the stirrup on the boot of Italy, so they were all closely related.

When the depression hit, it hit these people hard. They had no money to feed their families. My grandfather extended them credit. He basically kept all his friends and their families alive by carrying the credit. When things finally turned around, it wasn't like the next day everybody had jobs and gladly paid him back.

World War II is what ended the Depression which meant that the men went off to war. Not high paying jobs.

The net result is that most of the families attempted to pay some of their debt but most could not get it done. One family made no attempt at all. The head of that family used all of his resources to build a very successful business. He never repaid a nickel of what he owed.

When he became Grand Marshall one year, I was glad Dad didn't own a gun.

Chapter Six

Early Rituals

There was a comforting sameness to the early part of my life. Routines and rituals were the order of the day. Supper is a good example. We all had our assigned seats. Dad sat at one end of the table and my older brother Lou sat at the other end. The twins sat on one side and Mom and I on the other.

The first thing Dad would do is pour a glass of wine. It was a wine bought from one of our many cousins in town who had his own vineyard. The wine was pretty awful stuff but very strong; probably close to 25% alcohol. Dad always diluted it with water.

There were always interesting discussions. Dad and my brother Lou never agreed on anything and the volume would start ratcheting up. If things started cooling down, one of the twins, usually Joyce, would say something to get the fire going again. Mostly what you would hear is, "You don't know what the hell you're talking about" "Why don't you stop and think before you open your mouth." All this was going on while we were eating our main dish. What a lovely digestive.

Mom was raised in an Irish/English family. Food was not a passion like it is in an Italian home. To our good fortune she and Dad lived with his parents for a couple of years and Nanna taught Mom how to cook. Mom was a great student and she became a wonderful cook. The only issue she had with Nanna was garlic.

Mom used a reasonable amount but Nanna believed there

was no such thing as a reasonable amount. You keep adding garlic until you get tired of peeling and dicing. "Rita, dat's anot enufa da garlic. It don'ta hava no gusto!"

Our family ate well. Except for Janice who hardly ate anything. "I'm not hungry, I had a big lunch." Joyce would respond by saying, "No, you didn't. All you had was a Coke." "Yeah, but it was a big one!"

As good as the food was, eating the main dish seemed like an obligation for Dad. As soon as his plate was clean he would reach for the salad bowl with a throaty, "Aahhh! Give me the GOOD stuff." You would have thought he was going for a bowl of ice cream with a chocolate cake chaser! Salad! The man loved salad!

We had a large garden and grew three kinds of tomatoes, red, yellow and Romas. We also grew carrots, onions, zucchini, string beans, cucumbers and lettuce.

From our lawn we would pick dandelion greens. Dad would send us out into the yard to harvest the stuff before he mowed the lawn. Today if someone sees a dandelion in their lawn they immediately hit it with a heavy dose of Weed Be Gone.

I was never an aficionado of the greens, but I love a good dandelion wine!

Food and cooking were a constant in our home and remain a strong, warm memory for me. Dad's sister, we called her ZiZi, which is a corruption of the Italian word for aunt, was also an excellent cook.

Her children were Sally, Susan, Rachel and Peter. Their father, Uncle Press, died very young and Dad became a surrogate father, particularly for Peter.

Weekends and holidays would often find the whole clan, including Nanna, at our house. Three excellent strong minded cooks fighting over one stove; it was insanity in that kitchen. "The oven isn't hot enough for the lasagna." "I need to put the potatoes in." "Who's going to warm up the bread?"

The situation became worse when Dad's cousin, Uncle Lou, joined us with his wife, Mary, another great cook, and kids . They lived in a suburb of Boston and would drive down every once in awhile. I loved it because Uncle Lou would stop in Dedham, Mass, at the Dunkin Donuts and buy a couple dozen. He was always welcome in my house!

For two years, Dad would go out one Sunday a month on a friend's lobster boat. When they got back to port at three or four o'clock, Dad would call home and let us know he was on his way home with a couple of dozen lobsters. We would call Zizi and tell her to head over to our house with her brood.

Excited, we would put a huge pot of water on the stove to boil, cover the dinner table with newspapers, and melt two pounds of butter. Dad would arrive and we tossed the lobsters into the pot.

When they were done we would pig out! Lobster shells were flying everywhere. We all sat there with grease dribbling down our chins with huge shit-eating grins on our faces. What a memory!

Christmas Eve dinner was the best though. We would start off with spaghetti in a lobster sauce with clams, calamari and bits of cod. My mouth is watering just thinking about it. Then a salad fit for a king. What tied these two courses together was the bread.

Normally, two loaves of hard crust Italian bread were delivered to our door twice a week by Vorro's bakery. But holidays were different. Nanna would prepare the dough and we would take it down to the cellar and place it right next to the boiler with a moist cloth over the two big round mounds. About every hour one of us kids would go down to check on the bread to see if it was rising and re-dampen the cloth. Nanna made sure we turned it so the heat was even. At some point Nanna would tell us to bring the dough up to the kitchen. She would brush the bread with some mixture that included eggs, olive oil and, most likely, an unreasonable amount of minced garlic. Then, into the oven.

What came out was something from heaven: Golden brown, thick crust and chewy. It wasn't the consistency of sandwich bread, but it wasn't far off. The result was the bread went from being an accompaniment to a main dish.

Then there was the fried fish! Calamari, octopus, shrimp, clams, little silver fish called menhaden, and eel. All of them dredged in a seasoned flour (it may have had some garlic in it) and fried in olive oil. There were mounds of it and we would pick at it all night. When the evening was over, Mom would take the remaining fish, and there was lots of it, and pour malt vinegar over it and put it in the fridge.

On Christmas day it was brought out cold and we would snack on it all day.

Chapter Seven

Bright Ideas

Martha and I got married on May 23, 1998, one year after we met, we think.

We broke every rule in the book regarding maintaining a stable foundation for a fairly new relationship. Against all advice, professional and personal, we closed up our house, moved away from our friends, left our family, moved to a country where we didn't know one word of the language, the Czech Republic, and took on one of the toughest one month courses I have ever seen. A recipe for disaster!

I said we **think** we got married on the 23rd. Martha and I woke up on the day of our wedding and I asked her if we needed to bring anything to the ceremony. Martha said, "I don't think so. Why not call Lori, our minister, and ask her." Lori said we didn't need anything other than our marriage license. Oops!

We never applied for one!

"Don't worry about it. We'll go through the ceremony today and when you get back from your honeymoon you can get the license and I'll come over and marry you," Lori said calmingly. We got our license and had our close friends at our house two weeks later and waited for Lori.

She didn't show so I called her home. Her husband said she was at a K-mart blue light special. We called the store and had her paged. Twenty minutes later she was at our house. Martha and I stood in front of our fireplace with our matron of honor and best man. Lori said, "Martha, do you?" "Yes." "Larry, do you?" "Yes." Lori declared, "Then you are!"

The problem is that we can never remember what day we did the second ceremony.

Why did we pack up our house and head to Prague, Czech Republic? Well, you need to know my wife, Martha. She is an adventure junkie. Every year she comes up with 30 ideas of things that would be fun to do. Maybe one or two deserve a second look.

We moved to St. Paul, MN from Minneapolis. Our new home was around the corner from the largest curling club in North America. Curling is the sport where you throw this block of granite down the ice and people sweep in front of it. Martha decided we were going to learn to Curl. So we did, until Martha thought it was too cold a way to spend a Friday night.

When we moved to San Miguel de Allende in Mexico, a friend invited her to join the Croquet Club. This is the real thing, not the backyard variety.

At age 50, she decided to celebrate by enrolling in NOLS (National Outdoor Leadership School). This program is designed for people in their teens to twenties. You carry your own pack, make or cook your own food, find your own way and generally need to figure out how to survive.

This 110 pound lady carried a 50 pound pack and kept up with a group of youngsters for two weeks.

At age 60, she decided to bungee jump while in New Zealand. She was in New Zealand because she accepted an offer to run a Llama farm and B and B in Akaroa on the south island for eight weeks. Don't ask. You wouldn't believe me if I told you.

At age 70, she decided to learn how to play golf.

So packing up our house and our lives to head off to Eastern Europe to learn how to Teach English as a Foreign Language doesn't seem that far out of line.

How did it come about?

I was winding up a business deal and thinking about what I would do next. I didn't have to wonder for long. Martha came home one day and said, "The school district says I can have a two year leave of absence."

"Why?"

"So we can go to Europe and teach English." Of course, why didn't I think of that?

The plan was to earn our TEFL certificates (Teaching English as a Foreign Language) in Minneapolis, where we lived. After we were married, we would head over to Europe. Good plan!

Not so fast. After further review and research, Martha declared, "We will have a better chance of getting jobs if we earn our certificates in Europe and have a school help us find jobs. We are going to Prague!"

Martha then decided that the names Larry and Martha were far too dull for Europe. We would be called Lorenzo and Camille!

Our numerous challenges included selling one house, three vehicles and planning our second wedding since we forgot the marriage license for the first one.

Being utterly reasonable, we thought we should have a honeymoon for each ceremony.

After leasing out our house, packing everything up, enduring a seemingly endless round of goodbye parties we finally got to Prague! In line with Martha's and my new careers as teachers of English, the preceding are officially run-on sentences. It's a good thing this wasn't written directly after we arrived or we wouldn't have known that.

Our last 48 hours in Minneapolis were like running a gauntlet. We eventually solved the problem with the furniture that wouldn't fit into our storage area. Not surprisingly, Blue Cross screwed up our prescriptions. We were supposed to pick them up in the pharmacy on the southwest side of the city but they didn't have enough of what we needed. Unfortunately, they didn't tell us until we went to pick it up. We had to drive 45 minutes to another of their pharmacies which got us to the airport with only 20 minutes until departure.

Out of breath from all our running around, we figured we had it made. A great flight was made one hour shorter by a tailwind and a lot more pleasant by a double scotch chaser for a mild sedative got us into London feeling smug and refreshed. A short four hour layover and we were off on the last leg of our trip to Prague, or Praha, for those in the know. The Gods were rewarding us for our diligence and tenacity. This trip was a breeze!

Well, not exactly. Remember those prescriptions that caused us to almost miss our flight? Somehow they got lost between Chicago and Praha. Unfortunately, they got lost while they were residing in Martha's duffel bag which also contained everything she owned in the way of winter clothes, as well as a good deal of her summer wardrobe. In fact, she didn't have much to wear for the first two days. Thankfully, the bag showed up late Sunday night.

Our flat is a story in itself. The flat we originally rented was in Old Town Square but not available until the first of the month. We were assured that the replacement flat was much nicer but not as centrally located. The new place was south of the town center right next to a beautiful 9th century castle called Vyshehrad Castle (pronounced Vish-a-rod).

The apartment was on the ground floor, behind, and adjacent to a neighborhood pub. Patrons of this pub preferred to take their drinks out on the sidewalk where they could lean against the wall so they could place their drinks on the window sills. The walls where three feet thick which provided a nice shelf.

Since the flat had two large windows fronting the sidewalk, we would undoubtedly become well acquainted with some of the more frequent patrons.

A typical customer was in his late fifties to mid-sixties, male, overweight and with lots of scraggly facial hair. Because he spent the productive part of his life under communist rule, he was used to having cheap booze and cigarettes. As they enjoyed their vodka and smokes, we would hear their hacking coughs, plus listen to them ridding themselves of sputum. A pleasant background noise to our homework.

The Communists kept control of their satellites by keeping booze and tobacco easily, and cheaply available and making sure that any potential social leader was given a dacha outside of town so they couldn't organize and stir up discontent on the weekends.

These "dachas" were plots of land approximately 3,000 square feet with a shack measuring about 700 to 1,000 square feet.

Through marriages and sales transactions, some of these plots became quite sizable.

Situated in our flat, we were now ready for our training course. Classes started at 3:00 p.m., which meant we could have leisurely breakfasts on Wencelas Square with plenty of time to visit some fine museums before class.

Wrong, Wrong, Wrong!

Yes, the class hours were correct. The rest of it was fantasy. We would get back to our flat and have a snack before preparing for the next day. Around midnight we went to bed. We were up between 6:30 and 7:00 a.m. in order to finish preparation for class or put together a lesson plan for later in the week.

We usually left the house at 1:30 to head into town, giving us time to check at American Express for mail. We could also get in a short workout at our plush, but not overly ostentatious health club which contained two exercise bikes, some free weights and locker rooms no bigger than a walk-in closet. The best thing was they had a little snack bar where you could have a hit of scotch or vodka on your way out. If you were in a hurry you could just buy a bottle to take with you. Oh, get me a pack of cigarettes, too!

Interestingly, you can buy liquor and cigarettes at any retail establishment in town, even a jewelry store!

Anyway, I digress. School was intense. We had classes Monday through Wednesday. These classes introduced us to the teaching methods we were to use.

On Thursday and Friday, Czech students would arrive for us to attempt to teach them some English. The students were divided by their skill level: beginner , intermediate and advanced.

There were four one-hour classes each day.

When we were not teaching, we sat in the back of the classroom to do peer critiques of the poor slobs who were currently making fools of themselves. Each class was also blessed with a TRAINER who wrote the only critique that mattered.

After each class we had a lengthy feedback session. The TRAINER would ask the teacher what he or she felt were the highlights of their lesson. After this very brief recitation, the TRAINER would invite your peers to offer their opinion of your highlights.

Now understand, this pack of hyenas wanted to make points with the TRAINER. You are fair game. It was highly unlikely to hear a meaningful positive comment. Even Martha turned on me in one session!

You knew you blew it when the best offering was. "The students really liked your shirt."

You were then requested to share with the class your perception of the areas that needed further improvement. After this longer period of self-flagellation, your peers were again asked to share their wisdom regarding your class. Now these mouthy bastards can't shut up.

"You echoed too much." "You didn't put a period at the end of your model sentence on the board." "You peed your pants and everyone saw it."

There were times you wished you had a gun.

Then it happens. The TRAINER quiets the amateurs as he prepares to cast his pearls of wisdom. They are directed to take their places on your side of the table so they might better absorb his munificent sharing.

These pearls are the density of lead with sharp burrs. The casting is done in more of   an overhand motion. Reminds me of a baseball announcer.

"Here's the wind up."

TRAINER says, "you can take heart in the fact that the students really liked your shirt."

"And the pitch!"

TRAINER says, "Your lesson plan had the logic and planning generally associated with the Italian Army in WWII."

"He's outta there."

TRAINER says, "Keep up the great learning curve. I look forward to your next lesson. It would have been more fun to cough up a hairball than to sit through this last debacle."

Your faithful roomie and/or spouse has run home ahead of you and hidden the knives. If he/she really loves you, they bought you a bottle of Johnny Walkerovka with a large straw, because tomorrow is Saturday and you can sleep in till 7:00 a.m. Then you get up and go four metro stops to do your laundry. After that you run home to work on your "one on one," a case history of a Czech who wishes to gain the Nirvana of English speaking excellence.

May as well prepare a lesson plan or two, oh, and don't forget to study for that grammar test.

The rules to this teaching method are fairly straight forward. The students are to speak only English. The same applies to the teacher.

Since the students have a very limited vocabulary, the teacher must limit the instructions in a concise manner. Heavy dependence on pantomime and pictures.

We had two nuns in our class that had been teaching for 30 years and were used to standing in front of the class and talking away.

"Now, boys and girls, we are going to have fun today learning about the mating habits of Royal Albanian gnats. They are one of God's greatest creations!"

That won't fly (pun intended). The technical term is, "Too Much Teacher Talk." The nuns did not graduate.

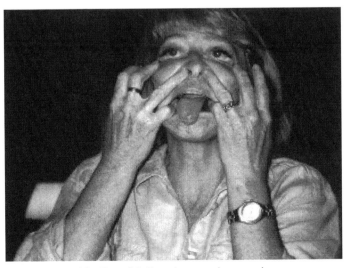

Martha didn't get enough exercise

Martha and I, hiking in front of the
Matterhorn in Zermatt, Switzerland

Martha and I out on the town in Prague

Chapter Eight

Vladimir

Before we left for Prague we were introduced to a young man, Vladimir, and his beautiful wife, Mercy das Sulcz. Vladimir was from the Czech Republic but worked as an engineer for a Minnesota based company. Mercy, from India, was working on her PhD at the University of Minnesota. A friend who was involved with the International program at the University got us together.

We gained a good deal of useful information from our meetings with them. Vladi asked us to look in on his recently widowed father, also named Vladimir, when we got to Prague. We did. He turned out to be a delightful, intelligent and enthusiastic gentleman. We had many fun times with him.

Vladi Senior spoke six languages: Czech, English, French, Farsi, Russian and German. He was an engineer and apparently a darn good one as he was sent all over the world to work on projects.

During the Communist era, the ability to travel outside the Soviet Union was considered a big deal.

Our friend stood about five foot nine inches tall with a sturdy build. His handsome round face was lit by a pair of laughing gray eyes. You had the feeling that the next thing he was going to do would be the most exciting of his life.

Martha and I decided we needed a car to explore the country. We enlisted Vladi's help. You would have thought I gave him the keys to a candy store. He started making calls to dealerships and he dragged us through several lots. He would get into arguments with the salesmen and tell us the guy was trying to sell us junk.

Finally, he said, "Larry, Marta, this is the car for you. Some small problems with the car but I fix."

After some back and forth with the salesman we agreed on a price.

Vladi said, "You stay here by the car. I go negotiate some more."

Twenty minutes later he came out and told us we can pay now. We paid the originally agreed on price and figured that he couldn't get the salesman to budge. We paid $700 for a 30 year old SKODA. Later, over drinks Vladi handed me the equivalent of $75.00.

"What's this, Vladi?"

"I told him he had to pay me a commission because you Americans were tight fisted bastards," he said with a full throated laugh!

Vladi loved to laugh. He loved to tell stories about how dumb the Russians were.

He was 17 when WWII ended and the Soviets took over his country. He was starting his college career but as the year progressed there were less and less professors. The Russians were rounding up all intellectuals and professionals.

"You see this street that runs along the Vltava River? We call it the smartest street in the world because it was built by Doctors and Lawyers and Professors," he laughed.

The Russians did everything wrong according to Vladimir except one thing. Every satellite country had one or two major industries that were to supply the Soviet Union. The Czechs had three.

"We built trolley cars for the whole Soviet Union. Our engineers say, 'Mr. Russia, I can make much better trolley if I change this or that.'"

"No, no, Mr. Czech. Don't waste time changing anything. These work okay."

Vladi said they did the same thing to a company that manufactured ejection seats for jet airplanes. The only business they would allow to do research and development was a company that manufactured an explosive called Semtex!

Vladi's other passion was fixing things. After we bought the car he took it to his house to "fix" it.

"What are you going to fix?"

"The engine, she makes a funny noise. I fix. The clutch she is loose. I fix."

After he delivered the car to us, he would call practically every week to ask how it was running. He seemed disappointed when I told him it was running great.

Finally, we made his day! Martha mistakenly put diesel fuel in the Skoda and it wouldn't run. I called Vladi and told him the situation. He came over within 20 minutes with a huge tool box. Five minutes later he declared that we needed to take the car to a local garage so he could work on it.

"How are we going to do that, Vladi?"

"Easy. You drive, I push. You go down the hill. Garage at bottom."

He was proposing that I coast down this winding, mile long street with about eight streets crossing it.

When I said I thought he was nuts and I wasn't going to do it, he was tickled pink.

"Is good! You push. I drive."

Two locals and I pushed Vladi and the Skoda to the top of the hill and sent him on his way. He was yelling with joy as he flew down the hill. We followed him in his car. Cars on crossing streets were slamming on their brakes and cursing him. Vladi never touched the brakes of the Skoda until he coasted into the garage at the bottom.

The best way to describe a 1960's era Skoda is to compare it with the Volkswagen Beetle of the same period.

One of the models was called the "Populars," meaning for the people, as "Volks" does. They were very light weight and underpowered with very few frills. As with the Beetle, one of the frills left out was sufficient heat.

Martha and I decided to take our first trip in our car.

Nuremberg has a massive Christmas festival. We left Prague on a bright and sunny Saturday morning to head for

Germany. Three hours out, it started to snow. As we reached the peak of the mountain it became a full blown blizzard. The car's heater was not up to the task and we were freezing. That also meant that there was no windshield defroster. The light weight of the car did not help with traction. It was a scary nightmare. When we finally got to Nuremberg much Gluhwein was consumed.

When we said goodbye to Vladi as we left Prague, it was a sad day. He agreed to sell some items for us, including extra tires and rims that had come with the Skoda. A month later we got a letter from him with a check for the sold items. He also told us he had a new girlfriend.

Chapter Nine

Seville

Prague is a beautiful city with wonderful architecture. The mass transit system is excellent. The beer is incredible. The people are warm and friendly when you get to know them. The food is so-so. All in all, a good place to live for a year. Well maybe not a whole year.

In 1998 the Czechs were building a nuclear power plant, which the Austrians were a little upset about. They were offering the Czechs a few billion dollars to not start the plant up, but they said" Zadny!" That means "No." It was probably a good long term decision for the Czechs. In the short term it meant Brown Snow for us.

The European winter can be bone chilling and damp. I grew up in New England so I was used to that. The difference was that in Rhode Island the snow was white! Without their nuclear power plant the Czechs coal fired plants stoked using their supply of soft brown high sulphur coal. The smog created by this coal caused health alerts every other day. It also produced brown snow. Not a pleasant thought and an even less pleasant reality.

Martha looked at me one night over cocktails and said, "This cold and snow is no fun. Let's get out of here."

"Where to?"

"Spain."

"Okay."

In preparation for the trip we went to American Express and got $800 of traveler's checks in the newly created Euro. Unfortunately the European Union had not yet created coins or bills for the new currency and none of the "casa de cambios," or money changers new what a Euro was worth.

It was really interesting crossing borders at that time. Because of the EU there were really no border stations any more. On one of our trips to the Portugese Algarve region, we both needed a relief station, (or Potty). We stopped at the Spain, Portugal border. Nobody was there. All the buildings were closed and boarded up. We found a secluded spot behind a semi-trailer and let loose.

For some reason Camille decided that we would live in Seville, Spain. Seville is properly pronounced "'Sah vee ya." Seville straddles the Guadalquivir River. The Tower of Gold sits on the banks of the river and stored the treasures that Columbus sent back from the New World. The Cathedral claims to house the remains of Cristobol Colon, or Christopher Columbus.

We arrived in the city on a Saturday afternoon. I dropped Martha off at our hotel and went to find our "free" parking spot. Two and one half hours later, after dealing with maps that didn't recognize one way streets, I found our designated parking garage. Unfortunately, I was informed that they were full.

I got back to our hotel an hour later and told Martha that we were leaving and driving across the Atlantic, back to Minneapolis immediately!

It turns out there was a cheap parking facility immediately behind our hotel. It didn't hurt that there was a great gelato stand on the first floor.

When Martha and I travel we like to chart our own course rather than taking prepackaged tours. This usually works to our advantage. We find great deals on obscure B&Bs or Hotels. Our Seville hotel was a three star. I eventually figured out that meant the size of the cockroach I found at 1:00 AM when I went to relive myself. No further need of relief.

We found an apartment in Triana, which is on the west side of the river in what was considered the "Artisan" section of town. The flat was a third floor walk-up with a balcony, one bedroom, kitchen, living room and no air conditioning. The key to surviving the summer heat is to utilize the steel roll down window covers and keep everything shut up during the day. Two fans also help.

A friend of ours, Jen Gemma, was living in town and hooked us up with her "job finder."

Non EU residents were not supposed to work in EU countries and it was illegal to hire non EU residents. Martha landed a job in a language school. On payday the headmaster would invite Martha into his office. He would look around to make sure no one was hanging around, close the door and surreptitiously slip her an envelope full of cash. I had individual students and was paid in cash after each session.

Fish Market

We lived two blocks from the fish market. It was in a building of about 7,000 square feet housing 30 vendors. It was always alive with customers and the sounds of the fish mongers singing about their fish and the prices.

Friday afternoons were special. The place was jammed, and not because we were in a Catholic country. The market is closed on weekends so the vendors have to sell all their stock. It would get crazy in there. One guy would sing out that his halibut was now 35 pesos and a stampede would head over to be first in line. Then another would sing out that his halibut was 30 pesos and the crowd would abandon the first guy and run over to the other. Another would announce his sea bass was half price and all of a sudden the customers developed a craving for sea bass. It was hoot to watch.

Martha bargaining at the Fish Market

The Beach

We were an hour away from a beautiful beach called Matalascana. We would drive and invite friends like Jen to join us for a day at the beach. One day we took Jen and another teacher named Jacquie. The day was somewhat overcast and breezy. We laid down our blankets and settled in. It was a great lazy day.

I looked over at Jacquie and her book was in her lap. Al Gore hadn't invented the internet yet so we still actually held a book and turned pages. Jacquie was sound asleep and she stayed that way for five hours. She was as red as a lobster. She didn't go to work for two day she was so burned.

Aside from watching our friends turn into crispy critters, we would walk the beach or have lunch at one of the many restaurants built right on the beach. It was also fun to watch the fishermen about 100 yards out. Their boats would go back and forth parallel to the shore dragging their nets. Around three in the afternoon they would beach their boats and dump their catch onto the sand. There would be crabs, eels, octopus, bass, blue fish and tuna. Make your choice, haggle for a minute or two, then put your fish in your cooler and off you go.

The Balcony

The evenings in Seville would cool down nicely and we would enjoy sitting on our balcony. It was four feet wide and twelve feet long. It had a roof formed by the balcony above us. I had bought a small BBQ grill and would cook on it on the balcony.

One day my neighbor knocked on the door and asked to come in. He lived on the same floor as us and we had exchanged pleasantries a few times. He had a very grave look on his face. He hemmed and hawed and finally said the other residents of the building had asked him to inform us that they were going to "denounce" us for cooking on the balcony. Apparently the smoke from our grill was getting into a lot of apartments.

I figured that meant that they were all going to shake their fingers at us whenever they saw us, or spit on the sidewalk when we went by. I thanked my neighbor and told him I didn't give a shit about being denounced.

He practically cried. "No, No senor. This is a bad, very bad thing to be denounced."

"Yeah right. What are they going to do? Call the cops?" I scoffed.

"Yes Senor. Exactly!"

Oh, so that's what denounced means.

I agreed to move the grill to a little plot of land behind the building and everyone was happy.

More Balcony

Martha's classes ran into the evenings and by the time she got home it would be 8:00PM. Jen Gemma came over one night to have a late supper with us. I had already cooked dinner and would warm it up when Martha arrived. When she came in we all got a glass of wine and went out to sit on the balcony. A half hour later I got up to get the dinner ready. Unfortunately, the sliding glass door had somehow locked. Oops!

Our balcony overlooked a small, lightly used street. Foot traffic was at best sporadic. Possible scenarios started coming to mind. How badly would I get hurt if I jumped? Thirty feet isn't that far. Jen and Martha are much lighter than me so either one of them would land a lot softer than I.

Or we could all take off our shirts and tie them together and make a rope that we could use to climb down. Nope. It wouldn't be long enough

Jen was the only one of us with any skill with the Spanish language. When anyone went by she would try to get their attention and ask them to get help. Most people ignored her. Some thought it was a joke. Finally a young man, about Jen's age, thought she was pretty cute and kept chatting with her. She finally convinced him that this was no joke and she promised him something. I didn't understand her Spanish, but whatever it was it got the guy moving.

Twenty minutes later three firemen show up at the back of the building. One of them got into our apartment by climbing a rusty drainpipe in the interior courtyard and coming thru our kitchen window. He unlocked the door and freed us.

Semana Santa

Semana Santa, or Holy Week, in Seville is a spectacular, spiritual and emotional experience. This is being said by an atheist so you know it has to be special.

Churches throughout the city all have sculptures of Jesus and the Virgin Mary. These statues are bigger than life size and clothed in elegant robes or dresses with gold crowns and jewels. They are staged to tell part of the story of the Passion of Christ. Those depicting The Virgin Mary are called Dolorosas, or Sorrows. Some of these sculptures are considered masterpieces and date back to the 16th century.

The statues are mounted on large pallets and protected by canopies. Some of these floats weigh more than 2,000 pounds and are lifted and carried by as many as 54 men who are hidden underneath by a curtain surround. This causes it to look like the float is moving on its own. These men are called costaleroes and each floats crew has a distinctive way of lifting, lowering and walking the float. The type of step they use is designed to cause the sculpture or some other element of the float to move realistically. I vividly remember one float where I would have sworn that The Jesus figure was walking down the street.

If the floats aren't enough for you, enjoy the Penitents and the accompanying bands. Each Church has a confradio, or fraternity, that organizes the floats and the bands and the penitents. Some of these date back to the 14th Century. The penitents wear robes and pointed hats with eyeholes cut out, called capirotes. Think KKK. The purpose is to allow the penitent, or nazareno to do his penance anonymously.

Churches begin their processions on Palm Sunday. This is a procession from the church, through the streets of Seville to the Cathedral and back. The trip can take up to 14 hours. Each church has an assigned day and time.

A church procession could include up to three floats, a drum and bugle band playing haunting dirge like music, followed by as many as 3,000 nazarenos. The penitents may be in black, brown or white, with distinctive insignias. Some might be barefoot. Some might be carrying crosses.

This goes on 24/7. At 3:00 in the morning you might hear the music, or the celebration as a church completes its march. But Good Friday evening is truly special.

The main streets of the city are lined with rows of seats 10 deep. The right to these seats is passed down from generation to generation. It's easier to get season tickets to the Green Bay Packers than one of those seats. All of the balconies and windows are jammed with people.

The processions begin at sunset and it is magical. Periodically someone on a balcony or down on the street will sing a flamenco type song. You don't have to believe in God to get caught up in the beauty of this scene.

As you can imagine, Holy Week draws tens of thousands of visitors. Every hotel room is booked and every restaurant is jammed. Holy week coincides with the National Convention of Pick Pockets and Petty Thieves. Kind of convenient don't you think?

Martha and I were standing outside the Cathedral watching the floats exit. It was a huge crowd. I felt something bump my hip, and then again. I reached into my pocket and felt this piece of metal. I grabbed it. A guy was fishing around in my pocket with a nine inch tong.

A few hours later we were walking to a restaurant and a guy came running by and ripped Martha's necklace from her neck and ran off. I chased him yelling LADRONE, LADRONE, which means thief. Shopkeepers came out of their doors and people were staring at me as I ran past. I eventually tripped. I gave up and started back to Martha. People stopped me to tell me of their efforts to catch the thief. Bullshit. Nobody did anything.

Two of the huge, gold and silver laden floats
that parade through Seville during Holy Week

No, this is not a meeting of the KKK
These are Nazarenos, or Penitents, that walk behind the floats

Chapter Ten

Fun Jobs

After I got my MBA from Harvard I went to work for Jewel Companies in Chicago eventually becoming the boys' toy buyer for the Osco Drug and Turnstyle chains. My counterpart for girls' toys was an older lady, Jean McPhee. She and I got along and she was a great help in teaching me the ropes.

We were considered a large account by most of our vendors and were frequently called on to go to New York or California to give input on new products the manufacturers were considering.

Aside from her husband, Jean loved Telly Savalas. She was addicted to "Kojak" and could recite every line Telly uttered in the movie "The Dirty Dozen."

One year, on Jean's birthday, we were in New York to evaluate a new product line for a vendor. After dinner we went to a nightclub. I excused myself to go to the restroom. As I am standing there doing my business, who walks to the next urinal but Telly Savalas?

After he is finished, I tell him about Jean.

"Could you come by our table and say, "Hi." "Sure. No problem."

I walked back to the table and pointed Jean out. He walked over to the table, tapped Jean on the shoulder and said, "Happy Birthday, Jean!" Handing her a lollypop, he said, "Who loves you, baby?"

It took her a week to calm down.

The International Toy Fair is a three week long convention in New York City. The official fair is one week, but the showrooms open earlier. When I was a buyer, the fair was held in the Toy Building at 200 Fifth Avenue and 1107 Broadway and connected by a skyway. The Fifth Avenue building dated back to 1903. The elevators were slow and creaky so it was faster and safer to run up and down the stairs which made the day long and hard.

Buyers are king for those three weeks if you have a "Big Pencil," meaning you are a large account. Manufacturing executives and sales reps wine and dine you. You get to go to the best Broadway plays, the best restaurants and the best nightclubs.

Too much and you end up exhausted.

It's also a grind for the sales reps. We could say no and stay in for a night. They can't.

One of my favorite reps was Jack Horschler. He was an independent rep and had some great product lines.

Jack stood five feet, eight inches. He was a clothes horse with a good solid body to show off his wardrobe. Conventional pinstripes were not for him. He could pull off wearing a lime green blazer and yellow slacks. His clothes matched his ebullient personality. Always ready with a fast quip. Always ready for a good time. One year, near the end of the three weeks, it was obvious that Jack's motor was running down. Jean and I went out to dinner and a show with him and one of his factory executives. After the show we hit a local bar for a nightcap. We left for our hotel around midnight, but Jack's factory guy wanted to stay out so Jack had to stay as well. The next morning, we learned he didn't get back to his place till five a.m. He managed to get one and a half hours sleep before he met with us at eight a.m.

The line we were reviewing with him that morning was a "peg hook line." The most boring job in the buying world. They show you a two or four foot section of cheap bagged toys which are referred to by number, not description.

Jean and I were sitting at a desk three feet away from the display. Jack, obviously the worse for wear, was in the middle ground between us and the display. He was wearing a powder blue suit with a lighter blue shirt and a floral tie in tropical colors.

When Jack moved to the display to pick one of the bags off a hook, Jean got a full view of Jack and she started laughing uncontrollably. She was so hysterical that she couldn't talk. Instead, she kept pointing at Jack. I finally saw what she saw and I lost it.

This impeccable dresser was wearing the suit, shirt and tie I described earlier. He also had on a left shoe of powder blue to match his suit and a right foot shoe of brown. To make matters worse, one sock was lime green and the other bright red.

Jack explained that he had to get up much earlier than his roommates and didn't want to turn on any more lights than was necessary. Combining that with overtiredness and a hangover explained the situation.

I enjoyed my time at Osco and learned a great deal. One category I took on when no other buyer wanted it was video games. I hit a couple of Grand Slams that got me major league press coverage in the trade papers. That led to me being recruited by several executive placement firms. As a result, I took a position as General Merchandise Manager with a company called Team Electronics, a division of Dayton Hudson Corporation, now called Target Corp.

Team was a franchiser of 115 stereo equipment stores spread throughout the Midwest and Alaska. Eventually this category of stores became known as "Consumer Electronics" stores.

Our local competition in Minneapolis consisted of two chains. One was Schaak Electronics. The other was a small chain called Sound of Music that was consistently in financial trouble. Sound of Music was owned by a very nice gentleman named Dick Schultz. I had occasion to travel with him to trade shows and factory visits in Japan. Dick was also a visionary. From the remnants of his small chain he built the largest consumer electronics chain in the U.S.: Best Buy.

Schaak was headed up by Dick Schaak. His father had operated a repair shop/parts supplier operation. When his father died prematurely, Dick dropped out of college and took over the business. Rather than closing it down, he decided to expand further into retail. Dick was a natural promoter and a charismatic personality. His retail stores grew rapidly.

He was aided by an advertising and motivational genius named Paul Ginther. Paul came up with innovative campaigns.

In the late seventies there was a product called a "Fuzzbuster" that alerted you to police radar surveillance.

Paul plastered outdoor billboards with the message, "Buy your Schaakbuster at Fuzz's." They owned the category.

Another creation of Paul and Dick's was, "The 24 Hour Sale." The stores, mostly in malls, were open from 6 p.m. on Friday to 6 p.m. on Saturday. Hourly specials in the middle of the night would draw crowds at two in the morning. One of the office managers, Mark Neiger, "The Human Hot Dog," would spend 24 hours in a bathtub filled with ketchup. Newspaper and radio ads would announce what stores and what time his tub would be rolled in.

I joined Schaak in 1980 as Executive Vice President. I had a good reputation as a marketer and administrator. Dick was looking to diminish his role. Paul loved what he was doing and did not want any of the administrative crap. It was a solid triumvirate.

The three of us faced a ton of problems with wisdom and humor. We owned a company that produced stereo speakers. At one point, when we had a huge factory inventory of speakers in the warehouse and slow sales, I ordered the entire inventory shipped to the retail stores. They had speakers everywhere. The stores were so crowded with speakers, people could hardly walk around. We put special prices on key pieces and spiffed the salesmen. The inventory was gone in 60 days.

Oleh Artym, was my Vice President of Merchandising. When he was working in the stores, there was no equal. He was great at selling the "Magnum 100." Magnum 100 was a stereo receiver and two 12 inch three-way speakers.

Oleh would engage a couple on the sales floor, play a record and starts telling a story, "Imagine you are in Spain, sitting at a cantina late at night. Listen to how the system picks up the high notes! The male dancer comes into the courtyard and taps out his message with his feet. The lady feigns interest and then responds; see her flashing her dress as she swings to the music and beats her feet frantically."

As he was doing this other customers would get wrapped up in his spiel and Oleh smoothly passed them off to other salespeople.

One of the most fun things we ever did was "The Schaak All Electronic Marching Band" that took part in the Saint Paul, Minnesota St. Patrick's Day Parade. Forty employees marching in formation with huge boom boxes strapped over their shoulders all tuned to the same FM signal. We had a van paralleling the parade route transmitting the signal. The music was "Celebration" by Kool and the Gang.

Paul and I led the group. We were at each end of a twenty foot banner with the name of the band on it. We would dance from one side of the street to the other. Every time we stopped, the band would execute some fancy maneuver. The crowd loved it. Perhaps the crowd watching the parade was heavily intoxicated because they never complained that the predominate color of Schaak, and hence our uniforms, was orange, a highly inappropriate color for the day dedicated to "The Wearin' of the Green!"

One of my favorite stories happened shortly after I joined the company. At age 42, Dick was about seven years older than me, and Paul was eight to ten years older. Both men were in superb physical shape. Dick was a state champion handball player. Paul was a large framed man in fabulous shape. . He was also a darn good racquetball player.

I played the game myself, but nowhere near his skill level. Paul kept inviting me to play a match with him and I kept putting him off. Then I had a brilliant idea.

I told him I accepted his challenge but we had to play at my club. He was fine with that but said, "Just don't book us into that court that has the glass walls." Of course, I immediately booked that court, not only because he didn't want to play in it, but because it also had stadium seating around it. I started bad mouthing his ability around the office. "Paul, you are going to get killed in this match. Totally embarrassed." "You will be sorry you started this." On and on and on.

Paul couldn't figure out what I was up to. But the trash talking was building the audience. On the day of the match we had about 50 people watching. Office people, spouses, friends and even my Mother-In-Law. Paul and I entered the court and started warming up. Finally, Paul said, "You have been big mouthing for a week. It's time to play."

"Well, Paul, I never said I would beat you. I said you would be beat." I turned around and walked out of the court. As I walked out, Matt Blair, the middle linebacker for the Minnesota Vikings and the NFL's racquetball champion, walked in. Matt was six foot four and his wingspan was enormous. He was also a fabulous photographer. Schaak supported his football camp for underprivileged kids. When I called him about this prank, he jumped at it. When Matt walked into the court, Paul turned around, looked at me and said, "You big Dink!" The crowd loved it. Matt proceeded to punish him. It was hilarious.

Corporate Officers

Top row/left to right: Bruce E. Yoder, Robert P. Zioncak, Loren L. Berg, Olen Artyss, Towru Nagano. Bottom row/left to right: Lawrence J.W. Castriotta, Joseph D. Osowski, Richard L. Schaak, Paul R. Giether.

Hope we get the right picture in the Annual Report!

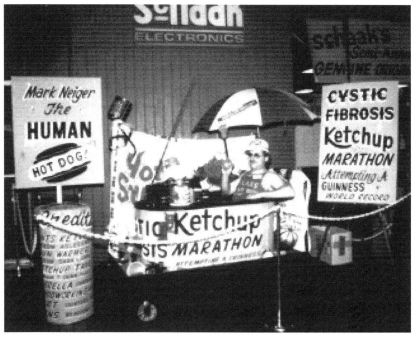

Mark Neiger sits in a tub full of ketchup for 24 hours

Potato Chips

When we were still in Seville I received a phone call from a friend back in the states named Danny Berenberg, "Larry, I have a friend that needs a CEO for a small company here in Minneapolis. It's in bad shape. You interested?"

"I don't know, Danny, we are having a great time here."

"Is it okay if I give him your contact info. His name is Nick Z. Just talk to him. Maybe he will change your mind."

"Okay Danny. Thanks for thinking of me."

I had done this kind of work before. Fixing small companies is a real challenge. The resources you need to make meaningful change are not always available. Sometimes your focus is to minimize the losses to the owners rather than turning the business around.

One company I got involved in was beyond saving but had several million dollars in commercial receivables, or money owed to it. When you shut down a business, it's nearly impossible to get people to pay you without getting lawyers involved. My job was to keep the business afloat until we cleaned up those receivables as much as possible.

An hour after speaking to Danny I was riding on a bus in the center of Seville. The windows were all down in this "Air Conditioned Vehicle," which made the ride noisy as all get out. My phone rang and the call is from Athens, Greece. Nick Z is on the line and I can barely hear him. "You want me to come where?" I asked. "To do what?"

After five minutes of neither one of us understanding each other I said, "Nick call me in two hours." I didn't know if he understood that or if he thought I was a blithering ignoramus. Either way it was all in his hands.

Two hours later he called to fill me in on this "wonderful opportunity." The company was a manufacturer of high quality kettle cooked potato chips named "Rachel's." Interestingly, that is my youngest daughter's name. Even more interesting, Nick's daughter was named Larissa, which is my oldest daughter's name.

Rachel's was founded by Jim Garlie. He and Nick Z were stockbrokers in Minneapolis. Nick eventually moved to his parent's home in Athens to set up a firm to manage money and sell mutual funds to prosperous Greeks. Jim was a good promoter, but not a very good manager.

When he needed capital Jim would turn to Nick who would come through with the bulk of the funds. Jim was pretty good at raising money from his clients as well. As a result of Nick's success most of the common stock and the bonds were in Greek hands.

One venture where Jim enlisted Nick's help was to raise money to buy a Canadian candy company called Triple C. Another was to pay for a sponsorship of an Indy Race Car. I later surmised that Jim was coming up with these ideas so Nick would keep money flowing. He needed it because the businesses were bleeding cash big time.

Nick asked me to fly in from Seville to Minneapolis to look things over. I did. It was a mess. Nick and Jim had raised more than $14 million and there was nothing left. The company owed more than $2.5 million and had virtually no cash. Suppliers were not shipping so the chip plant was ready to shut down. Aside from that, things were just peachy. I must have been jet lagged because I said, "Okay, I'll take the job."

I flew back to Seville and told my bride our European honeymoon was over. She was fine with that and started packing. "I'm ready to go home. I miss my friends," she said.

How to Lose by Winning

In early 1998 Jim decided that Rachel's should sponsor an Indy Race Car. Hell, why not. Got nothing better to do. In a creative and convoluted deal he signed a contract to be the main sponsor for Eddy Cheever's Indy Race Car two weeks before the Indy 500 race. The deal called for more than $3 million in first year payments and a total of $6 million overall. Nick didn't have time to raise all this money so Jim got the Cheever organization to accept shares in the company and the rest in potato chips, which Jim convinced another Indy car owner, John Menard, to buy for his retail chain.

Then disaster happened! Eddy won the Indy 500 in the Eddy Cheever Rachel's car. The paint was still wet on the car where the Rachel's signs were. The phones rang off the hook for weeks. We crashed our local exchange for five days. People wanted Rachel's potato chips. "If they are good enough for Eddy Cheever, our hero, they are good enough for me." It was nuts! Just one slight problem; the existing plant could only produce $3 million worth of product a year. That amount was already committed to John Menard and his hardware stores.

We still had our regular customers to take care of. There seemed to be no way to quickly increase capacity to handle this surge. Rachel's basically turned its back on all the new business generated by the Indy 500 win and still pissed off the Menard Group so that they dropped Rachel's as soon as they used up the Cheever chips they bought.

On top of that, Jim tried to parlay the Indy win into an opportunity to raise more capital by hosting big hitters at other Indy Racing League events. This cost the cash strapped company tens of thousands dollars it did not have and didn't lead to any significant cash infusion.

It is now mid-1999 and the company has no cash and lots of bills it can't pay. Nick leaves his home in Athens and comes to the states to try to save the company. This is where I come in.

I met Nick and Jim in Minneapolis, we negotiated a deal. I became Chairman and CEO. Jim resigned and Nick promised he will raise whatever money I need. The next four years were quite a ride.

One of the first things I needed to do was meet and greet our Greek investors. Off to Athens I go. Nick met me at the airport and drove me to my hotel. The streets were lined with thousands of people on either side of the street, all the way into the center of town. I waved to everyone assuming Nick had arranged this greeting committee. As it turns out Bill Clinton was flying in two hours after me and this crowd may have been for him instead of me. Just maybe.

My hotel, which is where the investor meeting was to be held that night, was in the heart of Athens. Most of Clinton's security detail was staying there. Anyone coming in had to go through a screening process. An entire ten block area of central Athens was secured the same way. As a result the meeting that was supposed to start at 8PM was delayed till 10PM.

I would love to report that the meeting was a triumph, but that would be stretching the truth a little bit. As soon as I finished my presentation and opened the floor to questions it got hairy. A somewhat upset gentleman of around 45 years, six feet and 220 solid pounds approached the table next to the dais and started pounding on the table and screaming in Greek. His rage was palpable. His sweat was flying off of him. I quickly realized he was not congratulating me on the success of my short tenure at Rachel's. I'm very perceptive that way. He was really pissed at Nick who had guided him into, what he considered, some shaky investments, including Rachel's. I politely stepped back and yielded the dais to Nick. Fifteen minutes later I was shaking hands with other investors who were wishing me well. Next in line was our table pounder. I thought about running, but before I could he grabbed me in a bear hug and kept saying, "You good. You good. Thank you."

It was almost midnight and I was ready to head to my room when one of Nick's people hustled me off to a car and said we were going to dinner with some investors. The restaurant was named La Cupia. You enter through a cave designed to look like a wine cellar. Every few feet was a cell featuring wines from different vineyards that offered tastings. Soon we were seated at a table for 24 to enjoy a 14 course meal with liberal wines and spirits to accompany each course. With every new pouring someone would get up and offer a long toast and point his glass at me. What's a guy to do? Drink up!

Nick delivered me back to my hotel at 5AM. He said one of the most important investors did not make it to the meeting because of all the tight security. We were going to meet him for a late breakfast at 10:00AM. Oh Joy!

Chapter Eleven

San Miguel de Allende

Martha and I built our home in Oro Valley, Arizona in 2001. We chose the Tucson area because it met most of our retirement requirements: No snow, no subzero temps, university presence, culturally alive and great hiking.

Not intending to move to Tucson for five or six years, we hoped it would give us a jump on escalating building costs, and it did.

Our first tenant was an Air Force Captain, his wife and a dog. No kids. They were model renters. When they left the place was immaculate. They even had the carpets cleaned!

Martha is a certified Early Childhood Special Education Teacher and a Speech Pathologist. She worked with kids from birth to six years old for more than 20 years. Early in her career, most of her students were Down's Syndrome or Fetal Alcohol Syndrome. In the last five years, her students were all Autistic. The work she and her team did was Saint's work.

When I would visit her class in September, it would be total chaos. By the time June rolled around, you would be hard pressed to believe that this was anything other than a classroom of normal kids. It's not that they "cured" any kids, they taught them routines to deal with their everyday behavior. The work was draining.

Martha would come home on Friday nights and yell, "Where's my Martini," and crawl into her overstuffed green leather chair. She was not heard from again till Saturday afternoon when she began weeping, thinking about starting all over again on Monday.

In February of 2005, Martha got a call from her long-time friend, Liz Powell, who informed Martha that she had turned in her retirement papers.

After hanging up, Martha said, "That's not fair! Liz is the same age as me. Why can't I retire?"

"Who says you can't?" I asked.

The next Monday she began the process for retiring at the end of the school year. We notified our tenants that we would not be renewing their lease in August. I got a call from him.

"Larry, my hitch is up in February of 2006. I would like to avoid moving twice. Any way you can extend us six months?"

"Sure, why not. We can find something to do for six months. For sure it won't be in the freezing cold Minnesota weather."

Liz called and said to Martha, "A couple of years ago a friend rented me a cottage in a beautiful town called San Miguel de Allende in central Mexico. I wouldn't mind going back there for a six month visit."

We found a great rental. Liz had a casita across a courtyard from our first floor apartment and large covered porch. The landlady lived above us. With that resolved, we began the process of packing our furniture and excess "things" and putting it in storage.

Of course we were bringing our 150 pound Bernese Mountain Dog, Mr. Rooney, with us to Mexico. We listed him on his travel papers as "Senor" Rooney.

BMD's are loving and loyal. They are obedient and docile, but if they decide they won't do something, you can't make them. We had one Berner that I was walking into our garage. At the very second he entered the garage there was a huge thunderclap that scared the hell out of him. He would never go in that garage again.

For our last night in Minnesota we had a hotel room on the third floor. Mr. Rooney put one foot on the elevator floor and it moved. He backed out of there and would not go in. I pushed and Martha pulled. She pushed and I pulled. Everyone in the lobby bar was laughing hysterically. Finally a couple of brawny guys helped pick him up and put him into the elevator. The rest of that trip to Mexico was spent in ground floor hotel rooms.

Mexico presidential elections are held every six years. In 2006, Felipe Calderone won a hotly contested race over Manuel Lopez Obrador. Lopez Obrador was a sore loser and claimed that Calderone's people stole the election. He was so pissed off he took the issue to the Mexican Supreme Court. He lost. He was still pissed and threw a tantrum, "They are all against me! I'm going to set up my own government!"

This was going on in September as we were arriving in San Miguel. We were dead tired after our long drive and some unpacking so we went to bed early. At 5:00 a.m. we were awakened to loud explosions like artillery. Thinking about Lopez Obrador's threats, I figured we were under attack.

"Get under the bed, Martha!"

"I can't. Mr. Rooney is already there and there's no room!"

The bombing lasted about 15 minutes. Seems like hours when you're hiding in a bathtub. I knew our landlady was up. I could hear her walking around upstairs so I went to her apartment, "Barbara, is this war?"

When she saw my pale face, she laughed hysterically. That didn't exactly endear her to me.

"No," she choked out between gales of laughter. "That is the Mexican way to celebrate the birth or death of a family member." Apparently, shooting a cannon helps the departed soul fly to heaven. Maybe the booming sound scares the shit out of it and makes it fly faster. I never did figure out how it helped a newborn baby.

I tried to explain that to Senor Rooney, but he wasn't buying it.

San Miguel de Allende is a beautiful old colonial town with cobblestone streets and ancient buildings. The main square is called the Jardin (pronounced "hardeen") which means garden. The design is like that of towns throughout the Christian world: The church on one side of the square and the government buildings opposite. Hotels, shops and restaurants on the other sides. Food carts and shoeshine chairs rim the perimeter of the square.

The church on the Jardin was called La Parroquia (par oak ia) or main parish church for the city which was the geographic size of Rhode Island. It is a beautiful structure of pink stone. People have said it reminds them of a pink birthday cake. The builder constructed it from a photograph of a cathedral in Spain.

There are benches placed everywhere to support the art of people watching. During the morning and early afternoon, the park is dominated by North American expats. There are upwards of 12,000 of them in the municipal area representing as much as ten percent of the total population. Being retired gives them the luxury of sitting in a beautiful park under a shade tree, wisecracking or ogling the lovely senoritas.

In mid-afternoon the Jardin is taken over by the school kids in their uniforms; the girls shyly flirting with the young men who are showing off their hacky sack athleticism.

The park becomes very democratic at night as it is shared by expats, kids, Mexican families and three or four Mariachi bands vying for the right to entertain. On the weekends the young people from Mexico City come to town and liven the entire city.

Why is San Miguel such a popular place for expats? Why did Conde Nast Traveler rate it the number one city in the world?

From a financial point of view, it is not the cheapest retirement haven. A comfortable house in SMA will cost between $200,000 to 400,000 U.S. That is in cash. Mortgages are virtually non-existent. Rentals are less pricey, but still not cheap.

Once your housing costs are covered, you can live pretty inexpensively. Two good friends of mine, Carol Schmidt and Norma Hair, authored a wonderful book titled, "Falling in Love With San Miguel. Retiring to Mexico on Social Security" They did it for six years or more until health issues forced them back to the U.S.

Dining is a highlight. From the street food to most luxurious restaurants, it is an exciting, mouthwatering adventure. Italian, Lebanese, Mexican, Brazilian, Bar-B-Que, Tapas, Pizza, French, Chinese, Argentinian, Continental, Mediterranean and Japanese are all available at affordable prices.

My favorite restaurant is "Taco Don Felix." Shortly after we arrived, someone suggested we go there. At the time the restaurant consisted of a horse trailer that had been converted into a kitchen. This was parked on the sidewalk. Abutting the trailer was a large tent that contained seven tables with seating for 25 people at most. It featured a shabby chandelier hanging from the tent pole. The other thing that was always there was a long waiting line.

Don Felix is a handsome man in his mid to late 40's. At five feet eight inches, his modest frame carries little excess weight. His sparkling eyes and ready smile set you at ease immediately.

As he walks you to your table, his erect posture and demeanor leads you to feel you are being taken to the Royal Suite. Dressed in a white jacket, he is a charming dignified host.

Mama and a helper are cooking away in the trailer. She yells greetings to people as they come into the tent. If the wait outside is too long, a tray of snacks is served to those in line. The food is excellent and cheap.

When business got too big for the tent, Don Felix converted the first floor of his home into a restaurant. He already had a commercial kitchen in his converted garage to support one of his other businesses. Another small room was converted to a full service bar. Business took off.

Don Felix, ever the showman, dressed his eight-year-old nephew in the traditional white jacket and red cumberbund and had him serve as the maître de. The boy took the job seriously, displaying his Uncle's charm.

There is an internet yahoo group called Civil SMA. After I saw the boy working the door, I posted a tongue in cheek blurb saying, "Don Felix is abusing child labor laws and he has his wife chained up to the stove and forces his children to tend bar and wait tables." A few people didn't get it and responded by demanding a boycott of the restaurant. The vast majority, 99%, did get it but played along. One poster suggested that we overwhelm the restaurant so that service would be bad and we could all write bad reviews on the Civil list.

Don Felix loved it. Business got even better.

I mentioned Don Felix's other businesses. He and his wife's primary business was the franchise they held for lunch at the largest High School in town. They set the cafeteria up like a restaurant with tables and menus. The students would order and be served like they were in a restaurant. Great life lessons.

Don Felix was also the primary distributor of cooking oil to the major restaurants and chains in San Miguel. He was a hardworking, ingenious entrepreneur.

Another favorite of ours was Ettore's. It was located in a permanent circus tent located under three large, beautiful trees outside the Fabrica Aurora. Fabrica Aurora is a large old knitting mill that has been converted into art studios.

Ettore was a tall, thin man with a long greyish/brown pony tail. He was a successful architect in Europe. His specialty was designing casinos. His passion was cooking.

I remember spending lazy Sunday afternoons under the trees drinking cool Prosecco made from Ettore's own vineyard.

Practically everything was made or grown on his farm on the site of an old hacienda about five miles out of town.

Ettore would serve a course of food, refill the wine glasses and sit down with us and chat. There were usually six to eight regulars every week. The meal would last for three wonderful hours.

Mushroom stuffed ravioli, roasted garlic and olive oil on ciabatta bread, rosemary pork roast, penne and chicken in alfredo sauce,spumoni ice cream. The meal was completed with Ettore's young, but fine cognac.

The entertainment scene in San Miguel was a pleasant surprise. A good chunk of the expats came from the entertainment business. These were performers who never had big parts, but made solid livings in film, television or stage. One of them is still active and has appeared in more than a dozen SVU roles. They are professionals. They are actors, singers, comedians and song and dance men. This makes community theater in San Miguel unequaled.

In addition, we had Beverly Donofrio who wrote "Driving in Cars With Boys," singer John Davidson who puts on a couple of shows a year, or how about listening to the great Doc Severinsen three nights a week playing in an Italian restaurant with two guys who he thinks are better musicians than he is.

Ken Bichel is an Emmy winning composer, producer and performer. He was influential in the development of the Moog Synthesizer. Ken put on solo shows a few times a year or sometimes hooked up with another accomplished composer and performer, Doug Robinson.

There was a 15-year-old talented singer living in town named Santa Claire Hirsch. Professionally we think we will hear a great deal more about her. She auditioned with Joe McClain, an opera impresario, who recommended she work with Ken who agreed to meet with her in his studio. Ken said, "Why don't you sing something for me?"

"Well, do you know, "You Are the Wind Beneath My Wings?""

"Yeah, I might know that. I was Bette Midler's Music Director for five years."

The talent in that town is amazing. I would say world class.

Joe McClain was a founder and managing director of the Austin, Texas Lyric Opera for 15 years. He and his partner, David Manning, retired to San Miguel. Joe's commitment to opera did not retire. He sponsored a Mexican national competition for up and coming operatic stars. The finals were staged in the Angela Peralta Theater in San Miguel. Full houses every year enthusiastically embraced all of the competitors. What a great show!

The city also features an International Chamber Music Festival, an International Short Film Festival, as well as a Writers and Literary Conference featuring authors like Barbara Kingsolver, Pat Conroy, Calvin Trillan, Gloria Steinem and Scott Turow. The conference now draws thousands of visitors each year.

I can't forget the Annual Chili Cook Off or the Rotary Club Super Bowl Party or the Feed The Hungry Annual Auction or the Casita Linda Annual Gala.

Don Felix making time with my wife!

Chapter Twelve

Settling in San Miguel

We were there less than three weeks and were impressed with the number of interesting people we had met. Why not throw a party? We did. It was fabulous. Bright, talented people, having interesting conversations.

The next morning, Martha and I talked about how much we were enjoying San Miguel and should we find a way to extend our connection with this city beyond our six month rental. We decided to look for a home so we could split time with our Tucson home.

We saw a house near our rental that was for sale. We called the realtor listed on the sign. An agent agreed to meet us there. Ten minutes later this six foot four inch, red headed guy in his early forties comes riding up on a four wheel ATV. In Mexico they are called "cuatrimotos."

We looked at the house but it wasn't for us.

Rich McClarty, the agent, said, "Let's go down to the office and see what else we have."

"Okay, Rich, we'll meet you there."

"No, just hop on in back of me. One of you on each side."

Before the words were out of his mouth, Martha was on the machine. I thought, "What the hell. I've had a good life!" I jumped on and held on as if my life depended on it. It did. Rich was flying through the downtown narrow cobblestone streets. I thought I was going to fall off a couple of times. Martha loved it.

After a few days, we found a great house that we fell in love with. It was on a privada or a small street with no outlet. The street was so narrow that only one vehicle could pass through at a time. You had to co-operate with your neighbors to get your cars in or out. When we turned into the street, I felt like we were walking in Venice.

Residents were a mix of expats and Mexican families. There were tons of kids.

Martha and I spent a lot of time with Rich and his exotically beautiful girlfriend, Claudia, as we worked to make the house ours. They both knew people who could do "things."

"I need to build a ramada on the roof." "I need someone to make a bannister for the stairs." "I need a good painter." Rich and Clau knew where to find them.

As our friendship got closer, we learned more about each other. Rich had been a very successful sales VP for a frozen food company. He retired at age 39 to San Miguel. After playing a lot of golf and ending a lot of days at the bar, he decided he needed a business to get involved with.

A gentleman in town had screwed Rich on a real estate deal so Rich decided to get even. The real estate market in SMA was controlled by the Mexican agencies. They charged seven percent and provided few services. There was no MLS. It was not uncommon to see properties with three or four agency signs on it.

Rich and a partner started Select Real Estate with a proposition that if you listed with Select exclusively, your fee would be 2%.

Taking an aggressive advertising approach in the primary expat newspaper, the company became known as Select 2%.

This strategy changed the structure of the market in SMA. Within a year, Select was the largest agency in town in terms of advertising, listings and sales.

When I met Rich he owned 50% and two other partners each held 25%. Neither of the other partners had any business experience which Rich felt was a problem. He offered to sell Martha and me half of his ownership. We took him up on it.

It didn't take Martha long to realize she wasn't cut out to be a realtor.

"They want me to work on Sundays?" "These clients are worse than my autistic students!" She retired.

When we decided to stay in SMA and get into real estate, the first thing I did was buy a cuatrimoto. Unlike Rich, I had a nice, comfortable bench built on the back of mine for my clients.

Selling real estate was a lot of fun but fairly frustrating at times. We would spend hours upon hours working with a potential buyer and they would turn around and buy from some other agent who showed them one house or some street realtor.

Sellers would list with several realtors and insist on the highest price somebody gave them. It wasn't uncommon to have a realtor tell a client they could get 50% more than we suggested. Invariably, the place stayed on the market until they priced it right.

Mexican sellers were a different kind of trip. If their house didn't sell, they would raise the price. Apparently, the lower price did not show proper respect for the house.

On the other hand, we had a situation where a really good offer came in soon after listing a Mexican client's house. They turned it down and raised the price. Go figure!

Despite the frustrations, the business was fun and lucrative. Clients loved riding on my cuatrimoto and many became friends. One couple, Ray and Michelle Arias, bought a home from me. Whenever they were in town, we would go to dinner. The first two times we did this my cuatrimoto got towed from legitimate parking spots. I threatened to stop going out with them.

Another couple, Darren and Mira, looked at a lot of homes with me. They finally found one that was three stories but beautifully done. The third floor was a roof top patio which was a common feature in San Miguel. What made this house unique was it had an elevator.

Mirra loved the house and Darren made an offer. It was not a good offer and the builder countered with a slight reduction from the list price.

I met with Darren at his hotel, figuring I had just wasted two days. I told him of the builder's position and asked what he wanted to do.

"Larry, I live by one rule in my life. Whatever Mira wants, Mira gets. We'll take it."

Chapter Thirteen

The Legal System

Mexico has an interesting legal system. The major difference from the U.S. is you are guilty until proven innocent. A few years ago the government passed a law reversing this but the changeover is slow. It requires a significant amount of retraining of lawyers and judges.

Another issue is the very limited power of the local police forces.

In San Miguel, the police could not arrest anyone unless they were witness to the crime or were directed to do so by the District Attorney.

We have seen this in other countries we have visited or lived in. If people overthrew an oppressive government, the first thing they did was severely limit the power of the police, who generally were the brutal enforcement arm of the regime.

In Prague, the police knew who had committed serial rape and knew where he was. They went to arrest him. He didn't answer when the police knocked on his door. The police left.

They are not allowed to forcefully enter a building

In San Miguel, Martha was walking home one day and two young men grabbed her purse and backpack. Martha is no shrinking violet and certainly not a victim type. She went running after them, yelling, "Thief, thief!"

A couple sitting in their car saw Martha chasing these guys. When one of the thieves was abreast of their car, the passenger opened her door and he ran right in to it and fell.

Martha's continued yelling brought people out of their houses and they chased down the other fellow. The police came and detained the two men. They also took Martha to the jail to fill out reports. She sat in a waiting area for three hours. She asked for her purse so she could get her cell phone and call me.

"Sorry, Senora. That would be tampering with evidence. We must inventory everything and send it over to the District Attorney."

"When will I get it back?"

"After the trial."

"How long will that be?" Martha asked warily.

"Oh, three or four months," the policeman said nonchalantly. "How will I get home? My husband doesn't know I am here."

"We will take you home after you give your statement to the D.A."

"How long will that take?"

"Two or three hours"

Martha did the conversion of Mexican Time to Real Time and concluded she was stuck for another five or six hours. It wasn't worth it. As soon as the officer left his desk she ran into his office, grabbed her purse and hightailed it out of there. She ran across the street, hid behind a bush and called me.

"Come and get me, Larry. I'm on the lam from the police!"

David Bossman, a friend of ours, is involved in a committee that works with the SMA police to improve security. He advised Martha to go to the D.A. office and fill out the complaint.

"We will send an interpreter with you. It will go really fast. They can't prosecute these guys because you tampered with the evidence but they want the complaint on record in case they come across those two again."

Martha agreed to do it. The interview went on for two hours. At the end they told her she would need to provide three witnesses to prove that the purse that was stolen was actually hers.

Martha lost it!

"I will have my husband verify it. If that isn't good enough for you, forget the whole thing!"

They said it would be fine. I went down there to identify the purse. I was questioned for almost an hour and waited while the attorney hand typed a statement I had to sign.

We loved our time in San Miguel, but five years was enough. It was time to start the next phase of our life in Tucson.

Chapter Fourteen

Horses

Horses played a big part in my adult life. During that part of my life, I met my best friend, Nick, I got involved in my favorite business and I eventually met Martha because of horses.

Horses played a big part in Martha's life, as well. That's how we got together.

I moved my family to Minnesota late in 1977. My first wife, Otti, had a cousin, Clancy, who was a Northwest Airlines pilot. His wife Jean, was a flight attendant, and a horse lady. She had an Arabian gelding named Mar Lindy.

My oldest daughter, Larissa, was obsessed with horses. She would go out to the barn with Jean as she worked out with her horse. Lara would then groom the horse for Jean. As a thank you, Jean gave Lara a Christmas present of riding lessons.

The trainers at the barn were the Kiesner family. Ginny Kiesner, a beautiful eighteen year old, was assigned to Lara. Lara developed quickly and it became obvious that we were going to buy a horse. Her sister, Rachel, also wanted to ride.

We became friends with the Lillyblad family who were also clients of the Kiesners. Their daughter, Sarah was moving up to a new horse and her Half Arab mare, Sherry, was for sale. I made a deal with Steve Lillyblad to buy the horse if he would deliver her to our house on Christmas Eve.

Otti and I created a treasure hunt that kept the kids to the far side of the house with the last clue bringing them to the garage, where Steve and Sarah were standing with Sherry with a big red bow on her. Their reaction was priceless. Something I'll never forget.

We participated in horse shows all around the Midwest. The social aspect of horse shows is a lot of fun. When the competition ends for the day, everyone heads back to their motorhomes or near the horse stalls to imbibe a few adult beverages. One evening, Ginny, our trainer joined us. Remember she was only 18, but everyone in her family was involved in training horses. Any trainer worth their salt knows they can't make a living just giving lessons. They have to make commissions on horse sales.

After an hour of chatting and imbibing, I felt the need for a rest room so I stood up and said, "I'm going to go see a man about a horse." I proceeded to leave.

Ginny jumped up and said, "You shouldn't do that without your trainer!"

"Okay Ginny. Let's go."

She walked alongside me jabbering, "Why didn't you tell me you wanted another horse? Who is it for? Are you going to sell Sherry?"

By this time I was walking into the restroom and Ginny realized where we were. She got red-faced and ran back to the group.

The horses from the Kiesner stable were transported by a company called Pegasus Horse Transportation. The company was owned by Nick Vangelof. He is a big fellow standing five foot eleven and over 300 pounds. His great sense of humor was infectious and it was easy to get to know him. We became good friends.

Nick is the only child of Dimitri and Radka Vangelof. They fled communist controlled Bulgaria in the late 50's. They spent several years in a refugee camp before migrating to Canada and eventually to Minnesota. His parents spoke no English so Nick did all the talking, haggling and arguing with officials and peers for them.

After one year of college Nick went to work as an over the road truck driver. Eventually he went into business for himself. Business was good and he soon had eight semis on the road.

When he got into showing and breeding Arabians, he set up a horse transport company as a sideline to help defray the costs.

Nick is a very bright, innovative and untrained engineer. He decided he didn't like the horse trailer designs that were available so he built his own from the ground up.

In addition to the big boxes hauled by the semis, he felt there was room for improvement in smaller trailers like goosenecks and fifth wheels that could be pulled by pickup trucks. Nick asked me to get involved with him in the business. I did, and it was some of the best fun I ever had. The synchronicity of the transportation business and the trailer building was incredible.

We would haul horses to a show and then set up a booth to show off our trailers. When we delivered horses to horse farms, it was always in a clean, relatively new trailer and semi. If the farm owner wanted to buy or build a trailer, we would offer to sell one of our rigs or build them a new one.

As a result, the transport company always had new trailers and tractors that were still under warranty. We worked with all breeds of horses, but most of our friends and customers were into Arabian horses. We would go to all the big competitions; the International Arabian show in Louisville or Albuquerque, The Canadian Nationals, The Scottsdale Show.

During the day, you watched the competition with your friends. At night you partied with everyone, and there were always parties. In between you talked about your trailers. As far as I was concerned, my work there was a paid vacation.

Chapter Fifteen

Motorhome Rallies

As I mentioned earlier, Martha and I belong to a motorhome club. The members are generally older but a fun, interesting group. Eight or nine times a year we go on trips or "rallies" together. On these rallies we do a lot of interesting things and go places we wouldn't necessarily go on our own.

As an example, we went to the William Hart Museum. Hart was before my time. He was one of the first cowboy movie stars in the silent film era that made a lot of dough. When he retired, he bought a hundred acre piece of land that took about four hours for his Hollywood friends to reach. With the growth of the county, it is now in the middle of the Los Angeles. Hart built a huge house of 12,000 square feet at the top of a hill overlooking the valley.

He lived in this mansion with his sister and his favorite horse. Yup, the horse had a room in the house right next to the master bedroom.

There sure was money in being a cowboy. One of our rallies took us to tiny little Willcox, Arizona the home town of Rex Allen, the Singing Arizona Cowboy. They have a Rex Allen Museum there to prove it. He was born and raised in Willcox and his family still lives there.

Right next to the Rex Allen Museum is the Marty Robbins Museum. I don't know why it's there. I asked the guide "Was Marty born here?"

"No, he was born in Glendale, Arizona."

"Did he ever live here?"

"No."

"Did he ever step foot in the town?"

"I don't think so," she said.

Go Figure!

We went to the Nixon Presidential Library in Yorba Linda, CA. Pretty impressive. It was built on the land his family owned and includes the house he was born in. It also had a Marine One helicopter that you could walk through.

Not to be outdone, Reagan's library is 100 miles up the road in Simi Valley and it has a retired Air Force One that you can walk through.

Next up we went to the Hearst Castle. William Randolph Hearst was a brilliant business man but pretty strange. The house is more than 90,000 square feet. That is more than two acres!

His father and mother did not have much faith in him and kept the family fortune, based in silver mines and Anaconda Copper, out of his control until his mother died when William was 56 years old. That is when he started building the Castle. Maybe his parents weren't so dumb!

The first structure in the Castle was 4,500 square feet of luxurious space that Hearst lived in while the Castle was built. One of the first things we saw in the main structure was a swimming pool about the size of Lake Michigan. That set the tone for the rest of the building.

Hearst had rules for all of his guests: "Drink all you want but don't get drunk. Dress for every dinner is formal. Do not sleep with anyone who is not your lawful spouse under my roof." Cary Grant was known to forget about the last one on occasion.

Sounds like reasonable requests. However, Billie's wife did not live at the house, but his main squeeze did! She was a booze hound as well! Don't know if she showed up for all the formal dinners.

We also hit the Nethercutt Museum. Like you, I never heard of this place or that family. Nethercutt's aunt was Merle Norman who started the cosmetics firm of the same name. Apparently cosmetics are a VERY profitable business.

The collection covers two large buildings that hold scores of classic cars, trucks, fire equipment, rv's and an antique steam locomotive. Additionally, the second building houses a collection of automobile radiator hood ornaments.

While I love cars, my favorite part of the Nethercutt collection was their Mechanical Music Instruments Collection. This included grand pianos, disc driven phonographs, player pianos, nickelodeons and a giant Wurlitzer Organ.

I'm guessing that Merle Norman lipstick that costs you $25 means a profit for them of $24. How else do you siphon off that much money to support this collection?

There is always plenty of food and maybe a wee bit of spirits

Even grown up children love Smores

Oops! Arches National Park

Chapter Sixteen

The Trip from Hell

Nobody ever said owning a motorhome was easy or inexpensive. Admittedly this most recent trip was a bit over the top. After you read this, you will be stunned that I said "most recent trip" instead of LAST trip and that Martha and I are still married.

To begin, we own a 42 foot motorhome we purchased in March of 2014. At the time we bought it, we also purchased an extended warranty for $5,000. Thank God! Or whomever.

So we were going on a two week trip to the Santa Barbara area to spend most of that time in a beautiful RV Park called Rancho Oso, about 20 miles north of Santa Barbara, CA. For three days we will be visiting with friends who have rented a house on the beach.

We wanted to get an early start so we could get to Palm Springs around 2 or 3 p.m. We left the house an hour later than planned and walked out to where our bus was parked. I hit the two battery cutoff switches and tried to start the engine. Nothing. I checked everything I could and even tried to jump the batteries with my truck. No go.

Fortunately, I had recently signed up for Good Sam's Roadside Assistance. (I am awaiting their notice that they are returning our money and terminating our coverage.) I called them and they sent out a guy about an hour later.

He tried everything but nothing worked. About a half hour into this, I was sitting in the driver's seat when I looked at the battery cutoff switches but didn't see any lights. Shaking my head, I realized I had hit the wrong end of the switches, the way our old coach switch was. When I hit the switches on the right end, the bus started immediately. Fortunately, the mechanic had tried some other useless attempt at the exact same time. I told him what a genius he was, gave him a $20 tip and sent him on his way.

We were almost three hours behind schedule, but we finally got rolling! When we arrived at our overnight park around 6 p.m., I started setting up; jacks down, power hooked up, slide outs out. All of a sudden I hear a sound like a coyote giving birth to an elephant. I could see all kinds of black rubber and smoke coming out of my air conditioner vents.

I guessed that one of my AC units bit the dust. Power in the coach was really limited. This was not a good thing. The TV's are not working. AC outlets are dead. Our residential-size fridge is dead with about two or three hundred bucks worth of food. Fortunately, the freezer had made a substantial amount of ice before it crapped out so we didn't miss our cocktails. What a relief!

The next morning we found a local repair shop. This was not a Camping World or La Mesa RV shop with huge clean bays and smiling clean handed service advisers. This was a dark dirty garage with motorhome remnants everywhere. It looked like a place old RVs came to die.

The owner of this fine establishment was in his 70's. He was skinny with dirty stringy hair and only a few teeth. As he sat on an old AC cover smoking an unfiltered Camel, he asked what the problem was. I told him I thought I had blown an AC unit and fried the electric system in the coach.

Hal got up and went into the coach. I told him it was AC number 2 of 3. He pulled the grate and reached up and undid a couple of screws. After sniffing around up there, he says, "Your AC is okay. You got a bigger problem." Turns out our inverter had blown up.

For you non-RVers, the inverter converts 12 volt battery power to 110 AC power to run things like residential fridges. Well, Hal bypassed the inverter which meant if I kept my generator running while I went down the road, the food would be safe to eat until I hooked up, plus I would have ice for our cocktails!

We left Palm Springs heading north. I called an RV repair facility in Ventura and he waited for us, even though it was Friday, to look over the situation. Yup, dead inverter.

We went on to our campground and checked in only to find that they only had 30 amp service in the park. We normally get 50 amps. SOOO, save the food or be cool. Decisions, decisions. Compromise: run one AC and the fridge.

Did I mention that when I was backing the coach into our site that Martha and I neglected to pay attention to a slope in front of us? Yeah, the one that ripped up part of the left side face of the bus.

Undaunted, Martha and I decided to head to Santa Barbara and explore the city. We were ten miles out of our park when our truck dies with a groan and a horrible smell; clutch. "Hi, Good Sam. I need a tow."

An hour later a tow truck shows up and hooks us up. Turns out the driver is a highly educated man with more higher education credits than an M.D. He lost his teaching job due to the California budget cuts but he was only making mid

20's anyway. Now he is driving a tow truck for more than twice that amount. Boy, are our values screwed up.

Obviously we needed to rent a car. "Call Enterprise. We'll pick you up." Except in Goleta, California, on a Sunday afternoon. They need a one-hour lead time for a pick up and it was 1:05 p.m. and the agency closes at 2:00 p.m. on Sunday. So Sorry.

Our friendly, over educated tow truck driver offered to take us to the Santa Barbara Airport where we could get a car. When we arrived at the airport, I purposely walked past the Enterprise booth sticking my tongue out. Can't treat me that way and expect I will do business with you again!

Next counter: National Car Rental. I signed the paperwork and got in the car when I noticed that one person was working the whole lot and handling Alamo, National and Enterprise returns. National owns them all!!! Can't win for losing!

The car had a keyless ignition. You just put a foot on the brake and push the starter button and off you go. I thought that wasn't very smart. What if I didn't lock the car? Someone could just climb in and take off. I'll tell you how I found out I was wrong about that.

The RV repair shop called and said the warranty adjuster needed to see the coach in order to authorize the claim. We had no idea how long this would take so Martha would follow me in the rental car. I started unhooking everything so that I could pull the motorhome out of our parking spot. .Unhook the water, the electric, and the sewer. Bring the slide-outs in, raise the leveling jacks....raise the leveling jacks....RAISE THE FLIPPING LEVELING JACKS. It's supposed to be fully automatic. Hit one button and up they go! NOT! We have had continuous problems with this leveling system and now

I am pissed. One flipping leg won't go up. I finally got them up manually and off we went.

After driving for about a quarter mile, I noticed Martha wasn't behind me. I stopped and waited a few minutes. Still, no Martha. I decided to back up and go see what the problem was. You guessed it!

Another unseen slope ripped up the right side of the face of the coach. A nice balanced look now.

As it turns out, you need to have the remote with you in order to start the car which I had in my pocket.

While we were waiting for the adjuster, we received a call that our truck was ready to be picked up. When the adjuster finished, we decided to put gas in the rental car so we could turn it in. The coach needed diesel fuel. Finding a gas station that has diesel and is larger than a postage stamp in sunny southern California is a challenge.

Martha was following in the car and I was searching for places to turn around. In the process of one of those turnaround efforts, Martha was behind me trying to make a turn in someone's driveway. Yep, you guessed it! An unseen low brick wall manages to crunch up the left rear quarter panel, GRRRRRRR!

We got back to the RV park and re-parked the coach without incident. Later in the day we went to play a game of miniature golf after which Martha took our dog, Maya, for a walk and I went back to the coach to start getting dinner together. Unbelievably, the damn door wouldn't open. I tried the key. I tried force and I even tried cursing but the flipping door refused to open.

After about an hour I found a window I was able to open. Martha had returned and I convinced her to climb through the window. The low edge of this window is six feet off the ground. She climbed on the step stool and lifted her foot as high as she could and just barely got her leg over the sill. I gave a mighty heave from the back to propel her into the coach. Miracle of miracles! She is able to open the door from the inside. I quickly jam a screwdriver into the lock so that the door won't close.

Later that evening, a fellow in the camper next to us came over to ask about the screwdriver in the door. Turns out he is pretty handy. He told me sometimes the inside handle and the outside get out of sync. He starts manipulating the handles like a chiropractor and, presto, the lock works.

Finally, we catch a break: No damage; no Roadside assistance; and no cost, other than a beer for my new best friend!

Everything was going along smoothly until the following night at around 10:30. We were getting ready to go to bed and I was taking Maya out for her nightly constitutional but the door would not open. From the inside! My new best friend had pulled out of the park earlier in the day. Besides, how would I get his attention? Throw knives and forks at his camper?

"Hi, Good Sam's Roadside Assistance. It's 11:00 at night and I am 20 miles away from civilization and I need a locksmith." A half hour later I get a call from one who wants to verify my location. Nope, too far! "Hello, Good Sam's . . . ." Around midnight we get a call and a locksmith is at the gate.

We toss Martha out the window so she can get in the car and lead him to us.

The locksmith is a good natured fellow about five foot seven and 350 pounds. No way could he open the door from the outside and I don't know how he is going to get inside through the window. He must have played some football in his younger days because he launched himself from the step stool, headfirst into the coach and did a head roll. The bus shook, plates fell out of cabinets and the dog's dish got upended, but he was in!

It took him less than five minutes and he had the door open. Maya ran out to quickly relieve herself. The locksmith jammed a screwdriver into the door so it couldn't lock and told us we need a whole new door mechanism when we get home. Out with the bungee cords so we can go down the road without closing the door.

Time to go home. I figured we could make it to the California-Arizona border on the first day. The ride is smooth and traffic is light. We should have no problem making it.

Unfortunately, we need to stop and take on some of that super expensive California fuel, $4.89 for Diesel, in order to get to the border. While I was filling up, Martha took Maya out walking. When she got back into the motorhome, she reached down and picked up the screwdriver that had fallen out of the door and absentmindedly pulled the door shut behind her. "Hello, Good Sam's Roadside Assistance . . . ." Two hours later we were freed from our coach.

At least we would be home tomorrow. We got a reasonably early start the next day and all went well. Traffic was flowing through Phoenix. I asked Martha to get me a glass of water. She got up and went back to the fridge. (Please, no lectures. I know it was stupid.) All of a sudden some jackass pulls in front of me and cuts me off. I slam on the brakes and Martha comes flying 25 feet to the front of the coach and falls on the floor. This time we were lucky. She ended up with a headache and some soreness but nothing broken.

I could say that was the end of the trip from hell, but unfortunately it wasn't. We had noticed that the truck was running pretty rough so I took it to my mechanic. After exhausting all other possibilities he had to conclude that the transmission and clutch EXPERTS that put in our clutch and fly wheel did it incorrectly. I authorized him to pull the transmission to check it out but to take a good video of it. Sure enough, the fly wheel was installed 30 degrees off so the timing sensor was not functioning properly.

I sent the video to the people who installed the clutch, to the shop that specializes in clutches and transmissions, to the people who have a kabillion years' experience, to the people who are certified EXPERTS. Their explanation was priceless, "Our mechanic said the flywheel was that way when the truck came in so he installed the new one the same way."

So if I brought a car into you with a flat tire you would put the new one on with no air????

You can't make this stuff up folks!!!!

Well, that was it. The trip from hell made up in equal parts of operator error, mechanical breakdowns and plain old bad luck. Can't wait to do it again!

Chapter Seventeen

Hanging Around with Old People

Hanging around with old people can be a drag or a lot of fun.

We were on one of our motorhome club rallies recently. I don't want to say the average age of our club members is old, but our youngest member asked how to register for social security benefits the other day.

Be that as it may, this is a great group of people. Many are retired military. Most are high achievers. We have retired Colonels, Top Noncoms, spies, former CEOs, aerospace engineers, skilled tradesmen and a couple of janitors.

Last night we had a great time. We are on a rally with eleven other coaches which means a total of 24 old people. During our communal dinner last night, the conversation got weird. After everyone showed each other's recent surgical scars, reviewed their most fun invasive procedures, such as colonoscopies or endoscopies, we began talking about other failing senses.

Hearing is the sense that nobody admits is a problem. Everyone can hear perfectly. Just because you answer most inquiries addressed to you with, "Huh?" does not mean you are deaf.

It may mean that the person talking to you is facing into a 3,000 rpm fan and the words are garbled.

It might mean that the person talking sounds like they have a mouth full of shit. Or you just may be deaf as a stone. Huh?

Martha tells the assembled ladies of the club, "Larry always says, huh, when I talk to him. His hearing is going but he won't admit it." They all pile on.

"Dave is the same way. He doesn't even say huh. He just doesn't answer," says the loving wife of another.

"My John has hearing aids but he won't use them," complained Edith. "When he does put them in he doesn't turn them up high enough."

It seems that every male in this club is deaf or hard of hearing. Not one female said they had any hearing deficit. Deafness is gender based! This discovery is historic.

Think what this will do to the marketing strategies of hearing aid companies.

"Hey, Guys. Do you want to be able to hear everything around you except your wife? Try the new ACME Custom Tune-Out hearing Aid. It lets you choose the voices you don't want to hear. No more listening to that whiney, loser of a son-in-law when he visits on holidays. How about that pain in the ass client that's always bitching about late shipments."

OR

"Hey, Guys. Want to look Macho, Successful, Important? Try the new ACME Show Off model. It's designed to look like a Bluetooth earpiece for your cell phone. As an added benefit it allows you to walk down the street talking to yourself! You are on the phone and closing a HUGE deal!

Available in black, brown or cammo for the outdoorsman!"

The possibilities are endless.

Memory is another favorite topic among the older set. I'd write something about this but I can't remember anything that was said about it. Forgive my bad joke.

What I concluded from everyone's comments is that memory is as selective as hearing. Yeah, some people have real memory issues, but most have chosen to remember what they want, and, more importantly, how they want to remember it.

Fact: Joe bought a new motorhome and paid $200,000. The list price was $225,000. As soon as Joe expressed interest the salesman said he could sell it to him for $200,000.

Joe says: "This sales guy is showing me all these rigs and I'm playing like I'm not interested in any of them. After an hour I tell him, 'I like that Acme Road Kill, but not at the $350,000 you are asking for it.' Well, it took an hour for me to get him down to $200,000 but then the tough work began. I made him throw in free air for the tires and a one month subscription to SiriusXM."

Joint Replacements

This crowd holds a Guinness World record for most artificial joints per capita. If we ever decided to take a trip that includes a commercial airliner, they would scramble every fighter jet within a thousand miles of any airport we tried to pass thru security screening.

We have artificial knees, hips, shoulders, elbows, wrists, ankles and jaws. Our medical waivers would fill a book the size of a King James Bible. If you're traveling and want to make your flight, you do not want to be behind us at the TSA line.

I must say that, given the average age, and assorted infirmities, this group is active and does not take shortcuts to handicap access. Those that do need to use handicap facilities use them. The rest go the regular route; maybe a little slower.

Did I talk about memory? I can't remember.

Balance

Old people fall. It's a fact of life. Why? There are a lot of reasons. Somebody trips them. Not funny, but there are people who get their kicks watching old people yell, "Oh, Shit!"

High Blood Pressure: Old people sit for a long time and then stand up and start walking. All of a sudden they get light headed and lose their balance.

Poor foot control: Old people's muscles weaken over time. As we walk, our brain says, "lift your foot two inches as you take a step." Unfortunately, the body says, "Screw you brain. I'm old and can only manage one inch." Welcome to Broken Hip Land. The place where old people start the process of dying.

Booze: It is understood that old people drink a lot. And why not, they have earned the right. If they haven't fried their liver by now, who cares?

Drinking leads to falling which is self-explanatory.

Incontinence

Nobody wants to talk about this, but why not? It's all over the airwaves. Depends, Aflex, Tranquility Overnight Protection, SCA Tena® Men™ Moderate Abosorbency Protective Guards.

Okay, we have male front and rear, female front and rear. Network advertising is only slightly less embarrassing than erectile dysfunction. What the hell does the ad with the two bathtubs mean?

Anyway, we all leak eventually, one way or the other. A million years ago it wouldn't have been a problem. We didn't live long enough for our sphincters or bladder to go bad. If they had, it wouldn't have mattered. Back then we defecated and peed wherever we were and no one thought twice about it.

"Yo, Grog! Nice dump! Can't wait to see the carrots that grow there next year.

Makes me wonder when the toilet paper business began or doggie waste bags. This is called evolution.

Okay, let's get specific. You are in your 70's and can control your bladder quite well. You urinate a few times a day. You have no "urgent" calls and you can usually empty your bladder. So, male front; no problem.

Male rear is another thing for you. You don't have big issues. However, there are times that you might have what we used to call "skid marks" on your undies. This is not the result of improper hygiene after an event on the toilet. You are experiencing what is called "rectal blow- by." Yes, folks, mix some exuberant flatulence with a somewhat age weakened fluffer valve and presto! Tire tracks.

Chapter Eighteen

Hospitals

I'm not sure if you are aware of this, but medical facilities are not a lot of fun. Urgent Care facilities are better than hospitals, because you can't stay at UC's for very long. Hospitals can be open-ended stays.

A while ago I was feeling terrible with major stomach pain. It started on Monday at midday and by Tuesday I needed to do something. Fortunately, we have a fine hospital in our town with a good Emergency Room facility, and an Urgent Care clinic about two miles closer to my home. In the last four years I have been to the UC facility three or four times so I figured they would have all my info, so in I go.

At the registration desk they handed me a piece of paper about 1/8th of an 8x11 sheet. "Please fill this out." Name, date of birth, address, contact in case of emergency, symptoms, phone number, alternate phone. Standing at the registration desk I filled out the form before handing it over to an octogenarian volunteer who then handed me another paper exactly the same as the one I just filled out. When I pointed that out to the volunteer, he said, "Oops" and gave me a clipboard with a two sheet form directing me to sit down and fill out the forms.

Before I left the counter I said, "You know, I have been here three or four times before and answered all these same questions. Surely you must have my records."

This good soul looked like I had accused him of assassinating Kermit the Frog as he said, "I don't know anything about that. If it was up to me I would have saved them for you!" Absolving him of the frog murder, I said, "Who can figure out these organizations."

As I sat down to fill out the new form I noticed that, again, I have to fill in my name, DOB, address, emergency contact, etc. Back to our frog killer I go. "I just filled all this info in on the first form. You don't really need me to do it again, do you?"

Looking like I hinted that he offed Miss Piggy to resolve a love triangle he was involved in, he quivered, "The first form is for me. I don't know what they do with the info on that form. You have to fill it out! That's the rule."

Okay. I fill out the entire form which asks for every possible malady or condition I, or anyone remotely related to me, has ever had.

"No. I am not now, nor have I ever been pregnant."

How do I answer, "Is your menstrual cycle regular?" "Yes, No, None of your damn business."

Do they really have to ask if I am incontinent? Can't they tell?

No beriberi, scurvy, rickets. No bubonic plague, Ebola or rabies. Yes to excessive flatulence, but that's fun, not a problem: "Pull my finger."

After wandering down this memory lane of past or potential medical horror shows, I heard my name called. A nurse invited me to an intimate little booth which felt like a confessional. "Bless me, nurse, I really feel like shit."

Instead of absolution, I get, "Do you have your medical coverage card?" Finally a truly personal interchange! "While I copy this card, please fill out this form . . . ."

I have now been at Urgent Care for 45 minutes, filled out three forms all asking for the same information and spoken to two volunteers who don't give a damn that I am doubled over in pain. Now I am sitting in the waiting area reading a truly interesting magazine named "Pancreas Today." There is a fascinating article on bile ducts. The liquid that flows through the ducts is called bilirubin. I think the Red Sox had a shortstop with the same name about 40 years ago.

This time when my name is called, I am led into the inner sanctum. In the examining room the nurse checks my weight. Why I don't know. I didn't come in because my pants were too tight. Then she checks my blood pressure which is not fair. Why didn't she take it when I first came in before I started getting really pissed off?

"Doctor will be with you in a few minutes" she says, and out she goes.

Two minutes, three minutes, nothing. I forgot to bring the Pancreas Today magazine with me and the only thing to read in the examining room is an article about the undervalued information in fecal matter. Bile Ducts or Fecal Matter; how do you choose?

Knock, knock. In comes Doctor Smiley Face. "Hi there, Clarence. How are you feeling?" "How the f.... do you think I'm feeling? I'm in here, aren't I?" Fuming, I say, "I feel like shit and my name is Lawrence"

He pokes. He prods. He looks up my nose, in my ears and disturbingly, gazes into my eyes. To break the tension, I tell him, "You know Doc, nothing up above my chest hurts, so can we focus on the pain?" Maybe that pissed him off because he left for ten minutes. Back in the room, he tells me I need to go the ER. "Would you like me to call for an ambulance?"

Unnerved, I say "Ambulance? ER? What's wrong with me? Am I dying? Should I call a priest?"

Dr. Smiley Face says, "Oh, no. It's probably nothing to worry about. Have a nice day."

Have a nice day? How? The day is half gone filling out forms at the "not so urgent" care facility and now I'm being shuffled off to the EMERGENCY room at the hospital with no explanation as to why.

At least Urgent Care has called ahead so they are expecting me. Hopefully this should be pretty quick. "Hello, Mr. Castriotta. Would you please fill out this form . . . ARRRGH

Unless you are bleeding profusely there isn't a whole hell of a lot of difference between "Urgent Care" and "Emergency Room." One difference is that you are immediately installed in the inner sanctum. Can't have you bleeding in a public waiting area. The magazine selection isn't any better but I found a copy of the bile duct article to finish reading. Fascinating!

I get the "Doctor will be with you in a just few minutes" routine. Why don't they say, "The doctor"?

Even the Catholics say, "The Pope," not "Pope will say mass in a few minutes." I guess in today's society, Doctor has more gravitas than Pope.

Even though it was a quiet day in ER, it took 30 minutes before "doctor was with me." What really pissed me off was I could see this guy schmoozing one of the nurses for ten minutes before he was "with me." She was pretty good looking but I know she wasn't in pain like I was.

Finally "Doctor" comes into my cell. He pokes, prods, looks up my nose and in my ears. Thankfully he does not look longingly into my eyes, but I do need to tell him, "My pain is somewhat further south, Doc." He looks at the results of the blood tests from the UC and sends me for a CT scan. Half an hour later I am back in my ER cell and "Doctor" is reviewing my scan.

"Oh, hmm, ahh, uh huh, okay, well then, looks like you're going to die in about four hours, so I think I will have you admitted into the hospital. Maybe one of our lunches can speed up the process. Have a nice day"

I don't think Doctor said I was going to die in four hours, but I'm not sure.

"Doc, give me something for the pain," I begged

"You bet. I will write up a prescription and as soon as you get to your room, it will be administered."

"Thanks Doc, you're a savior".

"Yes," he says, "I know."

All through this ordeal, my lovely wife, Martha, has stood by me. It is now about one in the afternoon and she is hungry. It doesn't look like I am a likely candidate for Red Lobster anytime soon and Martha is not a fan of hospital Jell-O.

"Go have some lunch. By the time you get back I will be in a room." Yeah, right!

You need to recognize that a hospital is nothing more than an overpriced hotel that gives you laxatives and bad food. A one-star rating with a thousand dollar a night price tag. Hell, I stayed at the Marriot on the Champs d'Elysee and it only cost me $800 a night, plus they didn't wake me up at two in the morning to ask me if I was sleeping well.

Check out by 11:00 am and check in at 3:00 pm. The room I am assigned is occupied by a hypochondriac with prenatal issues because his wife is thinking about getting pregnant. Leaving the hospital is not a restorative process for him.

It takes a massage therapist, a psychiatrist, multiple drugs, three orderlies and two hours to get him out of the fetal position and into a wheelchair so they can prep the room for me.

Finally, at 5:00 p.m., I was wheeled into my room. It's total chaos. A maintenance guy has a huge panel off the wall and there's a maze of pipes and hoses. He was poking around so I asked him, "What's the problem?"

"No big deal," he said, "we got a sensor telling us in the control room that there is a leak in one of our gas feeders in this room." I gotta figure out which one it is before I turn the gas back on."

"Maybe I should have them wheel me back to ER till you're done," I suggested.

"Nah. Like I said, this is not a biggie. Just gotta find the right one."

While this is going on a janitor is mopping up a big glob of something on the floor. I don't want to know what it is. An orderly helps me disrobe so I can put on one of those fashionable hospital gowns. (All I got at the Marriott in Paris was a terry cloth robe.)

A nurse is trying to insert an IV port into the back of my hand and an administrator comes in with a clipboard and says, "Please fill these forms out as soon as possible."

The nurse gets the IV going and it has some really strong juice in it. The pain subsides and I feel drowsy. Before I drop off I think I hear the maintenance guy, "Eeny meeny . . ." Nah!

A dream keeps surfacing where the doctor tells me I only have four hours to live. In the dream, I'm telling the administrator, "You can't count the time that I am sleeping. You drugged me so this time shouldn't count."

I won't relate any stories about hospital food this trip since the only cuisine I will be savoring is ice chips, without scotch.

An hour later, Martha returned. She is obviously unaware of my sentence of "death by ice chip," or the fact that I have only another hour or two on this planet.

Smiling at me she says, "I have been running around all day and haven't had a thing to eat so I stopped at La Hacienda and got this Chimichanga for us."

Morphine

Morphine is a wonderful thing. Trust me on this. It has amazing powers. I gained the power of flight. After testing my ability in my hospital room I flew down the corridor and checked the clock at the nurse's station. It said I only had 45 more minutes to live so I set it back three hours.

Did I mention that morphine also makes you invisible? I was able to sit at Doctor's computer terminal and double my dosage of this goofy juice.

Whoopee!

Back in my hospital bed, I was attacked by a bad guy trying to steal my blood at three in the morning Using my amazing morphine powers, I was able to think him away without lifting a finger.

At dawn all hell breaks loose. I think the night staff has been screwing around all night then has a lot to get done before the day shift arrives.

"How are we today? Did we sleep well?"

"Hell, no, we didn't sleep well! I had to fly all over the place so I wouldn't die on Doctor's schedule. Then I had to fight off a vampire. What the hell kind of place you running here?" I asked.

While this nurse was taking my blood pressure and temperature an orderly came in to mop the floor and a lab tech came in to take more blood and wants a urine and stool sample. All this happening before 6:30 am.

Nurse Jane says, "Doctor will be making rounds at 7:30."

I tell her, "Miss, I don't care what he's making at 7:30. When is he coming to see me?"

An hour later I hear the nurse talking to Doctor. "Your next patient is in room 330. He's the stomach," she says. "You may want to cut back his meds a bit. He is complaining about vampires and having to fly around all night."

That's great. I'm the stomach. If I had come in with diarrhea what would I be?

Doctor graces me with his presence. Doctor: "How you feeling?"

 Stomach: "Crappy"

Doctor: "Are the meds helping with the pain?" Stomach: "Yes. But I need much more."

Doctor: "Did you sleep well last night?"

Stomach: "Don't get me started! By the way, what's wrong with me?"

Doctor: "We think you have an inflammation of your Mahoney valve combined with an irritated Schinifler tensor. But we're not really sure so we're going to do more tests today."

Stomach: "That means I am not getting out of here today?"

Doctor: Not alive, anyway. Ha, Ha, that's a little doctor joke!"

Stomach: "Very little. Can I have something to eat?"

Doctor: No, You're in here on the airline plan! Ha, Ha, another little Doctor joke!"

Stomach: "Stick it up your ass, Doc."

Realizing he crossed the line, I was soon given another jolt of the good stuff which made the day more enjoyable.

The first fun event of the morning was I got to be Captain Morphine, a circus sword swallower. The technician put about 20 feet of stainless steel coil down my throat and swished it around.

The crowd roared, demanding an encore. "For his next amazing feat, Captain Morphine will take the same exact tube up his butt!" I was quite pleased they chose that sequence of events.

Next I laid on a gurney in the hallway for an hour or so looking up at the ceiling. Fortunately, Flying High Cinema was showing a really good feature film up there.

Something about Toto telling Dorothy, "Who gives a shit about Kansas. Let's get us some more of those magic mushrooms!"

Next I had a starring role in "2001 A Space Odyssey." I am in a cryogenic tube going through a defrost cycle. All kinds of strange noises confuse me.

I try communicating with Hal, our onboard computer, "Hal, are you all right? You don't sound good. Maybe you had some bad oysters."

I am told my performance was brilliant but to avoid the crowds of adoring fans I would be taken back to my room by way of the freight elevator. Such is the price of stardom!

The next morning is amazing. I am going to have a breakfast tray! The first course is the soup de jour; a tantalizing blend of water with a teasing hint of chicken. Next course is an organic, tasteless, gluten free, sugar free and calorie free slab of Jell-O. YUM! I am stuffed. I don't think I could eat another bite!

Doctor: "Well, your Mahoney valve is not irritated now and your Schnifler tensor is no longer inflamed."

Stomach: "Doc, it was the other way around yesterday. My tensor was irritated and my valve was inflamed."

Doctor: "Whatever!"

Stomach: "When can I get out of here?"

Doctor: "I'll write the release as soon as I get out of your room, however, there are stipulations I must impose: You must never reveal the recipe for our organic, tasteless, gluten free, sugar free and calorie free slab of Jell-O."

Epilogue

Well, okay, this is the end for this book. My editor says I am supposed to write something really pithy about the journey back to my roots and the existential awakening that this process has wrought. I would definitely do that if I knew what the hell she was talking about. I don't.

What I feel is, "Holy Shit, I wrote a book!"

I remember the book that made me a reader was James Michener's "Hawaii." The first two times I started the book I got bored reading about birds pooping out seeds to help create islands over thousands of years. Finally, one of my peers said to forget the first chapter and get into the main story. I did and I loved it. This friend also gave me a list of all the pages that were REALLY INTERESTING; if you know what I mean.

Look at that book! Think of the research! Think of the complicated characters and story lines! One person has the ability to put together such a marvelous thing as "Hawaii!" What an accomplishment!

My book is no Hawaii, but it is a book: And I wrote it.

The other thing I thought would be an amazing accomplishment was to build a house. Look at all the things that have to come together in synchronicity to build a structure. One of my junior high school friends was a guy named Richard Alegria and he built a house. He actually built a lot of houses and made a fair amount of money. In terms of achievement, I hold Richard up with good authors in terms of meaningful accomplishments. He's no Michener, but very few are.

I have enjoyed looking back at growing up in Bristol. It was a wonderful place and time. Because of the book I reconnected with people like Bob Evans, Mary McCarthy Panarello, Jan Russo, Steve Murgo, Jim Manchester, Dave and Rose Borgia and many others as I was "fact checking."

Bristol and its' people could fill another book without a strain. I didn't even touch on my nieces and nephews or go very deeply into my cousins. My brother Lou did a family tree and determined that when we were growing up in Bristol, we had 408 relatives to the second degree! Talk about a "village."

My first wife, the mother of my children, Otti, is an interesting, accomplished person and we had wonderful adventures while raising our kids, Larissa and Rachel. I enjoyed recalling some of the fun we had at horse shows.

I remember telling a young fellow named Josh Quintus, who was 15 at the time, who had done something to my youngest daughter because she was being a pest, that if he ever laid a hand on one of my kids again, I would break his face. Years later he became a successful trainer but wouldn't ship his horses with us. My partner asked why and Josh said he was scared of me.

I am very proud of our daughters. They are both successful professional women and, more importantly, they are incredibly good parents. Must be the great example Otti and I showed them!

I have declared an armistice with the Catholic Church, since I have recovered from my real or imagined damages done by that institution. On the plus side, how could you not relish having both Father Joseph Sorzano and then Father Mario Tardivo in your life.

As I write this, Pope Francis is conducting a hugely celebrated tour of Cuba and the United States. In his short time at the head of the church he has made it relevant again by putting a human face to it. He will not succeed in bringing the Church into the 21st century, but he is weakening the walls of resistance for his successors.

Growing old is another theme that has been fun to talk about. Martha is a great partner to grow old with. She is currently planning a one month trip to India, including working for a week on an Elephant Preserve, shoveling elephant poop.

Since I am still alive, I assume I will experience many more adventures before I "get out of the canoe." That means more things to write about.

You will have to excuse me, I gotta take a leak.

Interesting Sites for additional information

Bristol RI Fourth of July

https://www.youtube.com/watch?v=losxlmVf34w
http://july4thbristolri.com/index.htm
https://en.wikipedia.org/wiki/Bristol Fourth of July Parade
https:!lwww.facebook.com/bristol.fourth? rdr=p
http://fireworksnews.net/tag/bristol-fourth-of-july
https:!lwww.youtube.com/watch?v=Bzv1361IROk

Bristol,RI

http://bristolri.us/
http://www.explorebristolri.com/
https:!len.wikipedia.org/wiki/Bristol. Rhode Island
https:ljimages.search.yahoo.com/search/images;
ylt=AOS08xCuctSVZOAAnRVXNyoA; ylu=X3oDMTByZ
DNzZTllBGNvbG8DZ3ExBHBvcwMyBHZOaWQDBH
NIYwNzYw—?p=Bristol2C+RI&fr=yfp-t-608

Semana Santa

http://www.planeteu.com/events/semana-santa-de-sevilla/

https:l/search.yahoo.com/search;
ylt=AwrSbgGzcdSVTHgAncFXNyoA;ylc=X1MDMjc2NjY3o
QRfcgMvBGZyA31mcCloLTYOARncHJpZANEZyStNOJxbI
JNV2RaNzltVDZFamiBBGSfcnNsdAMwBGSfc3VnZwMxAR
vcmlnaW4Dc2VhcmNoLnlhaG9vLmNvbQRwb3MDMQRwc
XNOcgNzZWlhbmEgc2FuGEgU2V2BHBxc3RybAMxNgRxc3
RybAMyNQRxdWVyeQNzZWlhbmEgc2FudGEgc2V2WxsYSA
yMDE1BHRfc3RtcAMxNDQwNjQxNDgz?p=semana+santa+
sevilla+201S&fr2=a-gp-search&fr=yfp-t-608&fp=1

Schaak

https:ljwww.youtube.com/watch ?v=GyQi ngXbDsl
https:!lwww.youtube.com/watch ?v= TSdcM 6KD9To
https://en.wikipedia.org/wiki/Schaak Electronics
https://www.facebook.com/groups/61982803570/

29917355R00081

Made in the USA
San Bernardino, CA
01 February 2016